AIM FOR A JOB IN THE BUILDING TRADES

▶ **AIM HIGH** VOCATIONAL SERIES

Aim for a Job in the
Building Trades

DONALD F. DALY

RICHARDS ROSEN PRESS, INC., NEW YORK, N.Y. 10010

Standard Book Number: 8239–0203–X
Library of Congress Catalog Card Number: 72–110289
Dewey Decimal Classification: 371.42

Published in 1970 by Richards Rosen Press, Inc.
29 East 21st Street, New York City, N.Y. 10010

Revised Edition

About the Author

DONALD F. DALY has been in the mainstream of refrigeration and air-conditioning construction, service, and operations for many years, in close association with the technicians, mechanics, supervisors, contractors, and engineers in the field.

Born in Hamilton, Montana, he moved to California at an early age. After graduation from high school, he served in the U.S. Navy, the Merchant Marine, and the U.S. Coast Guard. He then attended a technical college for the study of refrigeration and air-conditioning technology.

After operating his own contracting business for a number of years, he joined a large contracting/engineering company as an applications and test engineer. This work included supervision, inspection, and testing of large installations for ships, industrial plants, and defense projects. He worked in this capacity at the Atomic Energy Commission installation at Hanford, Washington; the Reactor Test Station at Arco, Idaho; and at Edwards and Vandenberg Air Force and Missile Bases in California.

He is the author of books and numerous articles in his field as well as articles on technical subjects for such magazines as *Consumer Bulletin, Motor West, Southern Motor Cargo,* and *Overdrive.* He recently retired from active field work, but he continues to write for industry publications.

31258

Contents

Foreword

More than 3,000,000 skilled mechanics are employed in the building trades unions, including 125,000 apprentice members. Most of them are employed in the mainstream of the construction industry, which includes all high-rise office, apartment, and hotel buildings, schools and hospitals, homes, oil refineries, chemical plants, electric power installations, power and flood control dams, highway construction, and dozens of other construction projects.

Every residence, commercial building, factory, highway, power plant, flood control project, and distribution system that is built and put into operation must have crews of skilled technicians, mechanics, and servicemen to repair, maintain, operate, revise, and extend all mechanical systems, buildings, and grounds. The total number of men employed in that phase of building and construction is not known, but 2,000,000 would probably be a conservative estimate.

An unknown percentage of the maintenance technicians, mechanics, and servicemen are members of one of the building trades unions, but a larger number may be members of the in-plant union representing the production workers in that plant. A further large number of maintenance technicians, mechanics, servicemen, and specialists are not members of any labor organization.

The wage rates and fringe benefits for the mechanics who are members of a building trades union are among the highest for any equivalent skilled occupation. The wage rates and fringe benefits for technicians and mechanics who are members of an in-plant union are somewhat lower, but very good by most standards. The pay rates for technicians and mechanics who are not members of a labor organization vary widely. Those wages rates, however, depend to a large extent on the degree of education, technical training, and experience required for each job.

A career in the building trades and related occupations is not for every young man, but it is a fine career field, with almost unlimited opportunities for advancement. This book gives details of education, training, and experience requirements for many jobs on every level of new construction, maintenance, and service work, as well as information on wage rates, fringe benefits, and advancement opportunities.

Many things should enter into the choice of a lifetime work activity, not the least of which should be the financial rewards available. Wage rates and fringe benefits for many occupational fields are a closely guarded secret, but in the construction industry, in which contractors must bid for construction projects, exact information on such subjects as wage rates, fringe benefits, travel pay, and subsistence must be known before a bid can be prepared and submitted.

The following information on wage rates and fringe benefits for building trades mechanics was taken from an "advertisement for bids" that was published in a widely circulated newspaper. Such a bid request might list up to one hundred classifications of technicians, specialists, and mechanics, with a wide assortment of pay scales and fringe benefits. Space will not allow presentation of the entire list, but the pay rates and fringe benefits listed below for typical construction jobs have wide application in the industry. The wage rates and fringe benefits listed here will, in most instances, hold through 1970. (Contracts for building trades mechanics are usually negotiated for a three-year term, with increases spread over the three years. In recent years such increases have averaged about 6 percent per year.)

Classification	Wage Rates Per hour	Health and Welfare Per hour	Pension Per hour	Vacation Per hour
Carpenter	$5.68	41¢	55¢	17½¢
Cement mason	5.28	55	55	45
Electrician	6.30	25	30	00
Ironworker	6.10	30½	30	25
Laborer	4.14½	25	35	25
Painter	5.85	20	21	08
Plasterer	5.35	20	17½	34
Plasterer tender	5.02	25	35	25
Plumbers and steamfitters	6.42	51	50	50
Sheet metal worker	6.47	39	23	6 percent of gross
Welder	5.81½	45	40	22½
Tile layers (pipe)	5.05	20	00	20

Job Classifications

At this point it might be wise to define a few of the basic terms used to designate skill and training levels in the building trades occupations. Some authorities may not agree with the following rather general definitions, but as they are used here the intent is to show the relationships that exist between the various levels of training and experience. In most instances, the financial rewards that can be expected are in direct ratio to quality and quantity of technical education and craft training, plus the experience and ability of the individual.

Specialist: One capable of semi-skilled work activity that can be mastered in a limited time.

Technician: One who can handle work activity that requires technical education of one year duration, plus on-the-job work experience.

Technologist: This term might apply to anyone prepared for work activity that requires two years of trade school education, plus on-the-job experience.

Associate in Science: One who has completed the two-year, college-level course of education and training earning a student an Associate in Science Degree in building trades technology. It includes such subjects as air conditioning and refrigeration, drafting, instrumentation, and building maintenance. This level of technical education has very wide application in the building trades and can form the basis for a very rewarding career.

Apprenticeship: This method of training is common in the building trades and requires from four to five years of classroom study and on-the-job work activity. A completed apprenticeship means graduation to the journeyman level and the opportunity for a rewarding lifetime career.

Journeyman: The journeyman level of training is superior to any classification listed so far. It is the basic skill level for qualified mechanics in the building trades, and many men use it as a steppingstone to jobs as supervisors, estimators, instructors, and to ownership of a successful contracting business.

Master Mechanic: Under present laws in many states, the owner and operator of a contracting business for the building trades must pass an examination to prove that he has the knowledge, experience, and ability to operate such a business. The title of Master Mechanic could also be applied to a journeyman mechanic who has demonstrated the ability to supervise work activities of apprentice and journeymen mechanics of his craft. On a higher supervisory level the Master Mechanic may be required to supervise work activities of all building trades craftsmen employed on a construction project.

*   *   *   *   *

Note: The purpose of this book is to give the student-trainee information that will make it possible for him to evaluate career opportunities in the building and construction trades. It is *not* the purpose of this book to make out a case for, or against, union membership. That question must be decided by each individual.

AIM FOR A JOB IN THE BUILDING TRADES

CHAPTER I

A Trade Is an Estate

A very wise and successful man once said, "A man who has a trade has an estate." A little reflection will convince even the skeptics of the truth of that statement, but most of us think of an estate in terms of real estate, stocks and bonds, personal property, or money in the bank. The truth is that the most valuable property most men will ever own is the education, knowledge, experience, and skills they have acquired in their trade or profession.

That fact becomes obvious when we consider the actions of partners in a successful business enterprise, or the officers of a corporation, when they insure the lives of partners or executives for large sums of money. Those officials know the value of experience and training and understand that the loss of a key man could be a shattering blow to any business. Those partners and high level executives have one thing in common with a man who has mastered a trade—both have a valuable property in their experience, skill, and know-how.

If every man would seek to create an estate in his vocation and would use the same care in building a vocation that he would use in building an estate of property, he would be very wise indeed. Most of us use good judgment when we set out to accumulate an estate of property. We are thrifty and we put our savings to work at interest. We keep our home in good repair, and the lawn and shrubbery neatly trimmed. We do so because we know that such care will enhance the value of the property. A wise man will take the same attitude toward the chief asset he will ever own—his trade or profession.

17

The average building trades mechanic will, according to the best available statistics, enter an apprenticeship (formal or informal) between the ages of 18 and 21. That means he will graduate to journeyman mechanic not later than at age 25. The same statistics indicate that most men will continue to work at their chosen profession until they retire. The present age for retirement is considered to be 65, which means that the average mechanic will work at his trade for forty years, and that his lifetime earnings will be in excess of $400,000. That figure may seem high by past standards, but it is probably much too conservative.

The lifetime earning potential for a mechanic in the building trades, by comparison with the earning potential of men on other educational levels, is illustrated by the following table. (Information is based on the best available statistics.)

Educational Level	Lifetime Earnings Potential
Grammar-School Graduate	$156,000
High-School Graduate	$246,000
College Graduate B.A.	$440,000
Building Trades Journeyman	$400,000

The fact that a man serves an apprenticeship and graduates to journeyman mechanic does not mean he will be limited to the journeyman level of work activity. On the contrary, many men use the knowledge and experience they have gained by working at their trade as a steppingstone to better things. Every ambitious building trades mechanic will have many chances to move up to a job as estimator, inspector, shop foreman, superintendent, or to the ownership of his own contracting business.

Because of such advancement potential, a good mechanic will have respect for his trade and will make every effort to protect and increase the value of the investment he has in his chosen vocation. Only a fool would allow a piece of rental property, or his home, to depreciate to the extent that it would not bring a fair return on the investment or appreciate in value, and only a fool would allow his skill at his trade to depreciate to the extent that he becomes an inferior craftsman.

Every building trades craftsman can do many things to enhance the value of his vocation. He can add to his knowledge by taking such courses as shop mathematics, mechanical drawing, or blueprint reading, but he should not confine his learning to the mechanical aspects of his trade. The study of other apparently unrelated subjects such as applied psychology, supervisory methods, personal development, reading comprehension, and so forth can lay the groundwork for promotion, greater career satisfaction, and fulfillment. Graduation from high school, or from an apprenticeship, should not mean the end of learning. It should mean that a foundation has been laid for the real education that will come with experience and maturity.

Questions and Answers

Q. Why should a man who has mastered one of the building trades feel that he has an estate in that trade?

A. Because the knowledge, experience, and skill he has in his trade will be his chief asset and main source of income.

Q. How can a building trades craftsman increase the value of the estate he has in his trade?

A. By keeping up with new developments in his field and continuing his technical education. The more varied his skills the more his services will be in demand.

Q. There are many special jobs in the building trades. Would it be wise for an apprentice to concentrate on one of those specialties, rather than try to master the entire trade?

A. No, a specialist is extremely limited when it comes to jobs and advancement. The services of a fully qualified journeyman are always in demand.

Q. If an apprentice completes his training and graduates to the journeyman level, how long can he expect to work at his trade?

A. There is much evidence to indicate that most men who have completed an apprenticeship continue to work at that trade until retirement.

Q. Would one of the building trades occupations be a good lifetime vocation?

A. Yes, that would be a fine career choice. Few fields offer the variety of work and the opportunities for advancement that are found in building and construction.

Q. Would a building trades apprentice be better off if he did not belong to a labor union?

A. No. Those unions have fine training programs, plus excellent wages, fringe benefits, and fine working conditions.

Q. How does the earning potential for building trades craftsmen compare with the earning potential for other occupational fields?

A. The earning potential compares very well with all other jobs that require equivalent skills. It is exceeded only by the jobs that require a college degree.

Q. Are there more jobs in the building and construction trades than there were twenty years ago?

A. Yes. Many more jobs are available, and the skill requirements for most jobs are higher than those of twenty years ago. It seems obvious that the trend toward more jobs that require a higher degree of skill will last into the forseeable future.

Q. Are the fringe benefits that mechanics of the building trades receive under their union contracts an important part of their total yearly earnings?

A. Yes. In many instances the fringe benefits amount to as much as 10 percent of gross pay, but that does not tell the entire story. Much better coverage is available under group insurance than would be available to the individual. Fringe benefits can include up to three weeks' vacation each year; holiday pay; health and welfare insurance; group life insurance; and a pension. Most benefits include all dependents.

CHAPTER II

Job Opportunities

Some of the finest jobs available today are in the construction industry and the best of those jobs are under the jurisdiction of the building trades unions. Some critics have charged that those unions have a monopoly on construction jobs, but that charge would be hard to substantiate. It is possible that some of the unions have tried to foster that idea, but no such monopoly could exist under present-day labor laws.

The purpose of every building trades union is to serve the community in which it operates, and it accomplishes that purpose by training and making available to that community a pool of skilled craftsmen. On the whole the unions do a good job, often at the cost of bitter criticism from their own members and the general public.

They try to select the best men available for those trades, but there is some truth to the charge that many men who have the experience and the skill to qualify never have a chance to become members. That does not happen, however, because those unions have monopolistic control of jobs; it happens because a great many prospective members do not understand how the unions operate.

Good jobs are unquestionably available in the construction industry. A journeyman mechanic, if he is well qualified, can expect to earn from $10,000 to $12,000 a year. A foreman or general foreman can expect to earn up to $16,000 a year. Many mechanics, after a few years of seasoning, move up to the ownership of their own contracting business.

It is a sad thing that lack of knowledge of the operation of the unions can mean that men with all of the needed qualifications for success may never achieve it, for the simple reason that they never take the first step—to become a member of the building trades union for their trade. Two distinct groups of men would be well advised to seek membership in one of the building trades unions:

1. The Apprentice Candidate for Membership
The first group includes men between the ages of 18 and 25 who might be eligible for an apprenticeship. To qualify as an apprentice for most trades a man must have a high-school education, a clear record, and a sponsor. The sponsor may be any reputable member of the community, a member of the union who is in good standing, or a contractor who is signatory to an agreement with that union.

The apprentice candidate need not have had previous experience in the trade of his choice, but such experience can be very helpful. In fact, if the candidate has had experience that can be verified, he might be able to get credit against the five-year apprenticeship. If the candidate has completed a meaningful amount of trade-school work, such experience may help his chances for acceptance as an apprentice.

2. The Journeyman Candidate for Membership
Most of the men in this group will be past the age to gain membership through an apprenticeship. Such candidates may have gained experience at a trade while working in nonunion shops, on service work, maintenance and repair, or in an industrial plant where men with these skills are employed. Many of them may have been members of an in-plant union, and such membership can be an asset.

These plumbers, pipefitters, painters, electricians, sheet metal workers, millrights, carpenters, and the like are often skilled in a special branch of a trade. Their skill will often be of a nature to place them on the semiskilled or technician level. Jobs on that level offer little chance for advancement, and an ambitious man will not be content to remain there. It has been proved many times that many of those men could qualify for membership in a building trades union.

Any mechanic who has such a level of training and experience and believes that he can qualify, should simply go to the office of the building trades union that has jurisdiction over his trade and make application for membership. He will be required to prove that he has had five years of experience at his trade. That may include experience gained while working as a helper, apprentice, or journeyman, or any special classification.

The proof of experience can be in the form of letters from former employers or sworn affidavits made by responsible individuals who have knowledge of the candidate's experience. All such letters are much more effective if they are on the official letterhead of an established company that is known to employ craftsmen of the trade in question. Every candidate is subjected to a thorough investigation, which means that it would not be wise to present false credentials.

If the evidence stands up under investigation, the candidate will be required to take an examination to determine the extent and quality of his experience. The examination will combine written and oral questions and will be similar in nature to examinations that are given for equivalent jobs in civil service. The examination will not be easy, but it will be fair. The minimum passing grade is 70 percent, and any candidate who achieves that grade will be accepted as a member.

Any man who seeks membership in one of the building trades unions, on either the apprentice or the journeyman level, should understand the need to be persistent in his effort. If a man is rebuffed on his first visit to the union office he should not be discouraged and should not give up. If a journeyman candidate fails to pass the examination on his first try he should go back and try again later. The number of times a candidate is allowed

A steam-generating plant being erected at a cost of $132,000,000, with a planned capacity of 2,114,000 kilowatts.

to take the examination is unlimited, but in some instances a waiting period of from three to six months is required to give a candidate a chance to study and gain additional experience. The building trades unions have many problems. They must maintain a membership large enough to meet all demands for skilled craftsmen, but they must not allow the membership to become so large that skilled men will leave the trade when work is slack. Even under the most favorable employment conditions, the better-qualified mechanics in the building trades tend to flow through the unions to jobs on the management level.

The building and construction industry includes many trades and many specialties, and each union has its own jurisdiction of work and territory. The methods used to select and examine men for membership will vary somewhat from one union to another, and from one section of the country to another.

The reception a candidate, either apprentice or journeyman, receives when he goes to a union office to apply for membership depends on a number of factors, including the local labor supply, activity in the local construction industry, and the state of business in general. In any case, the best place to get information on the subject, or to make application for membership, is the office of the local union for the specific trade of interest. The unions are listed in city directories and telephone books.

Questions and Answers

Q. Do the building trades unions have absolute control over jobs in the construction industry?

A. No. A monopoly of that sort would be impossible under existing labor laws. Membership in these unions is open to anyone who has the training, experience, and skill to qualify.

Q. Do those unions try to hold down membership in an effort to create a false shortage of building trades craftsmen?

A. No. The unions are constantly seeking to increase their memberships and to extend the jurisdiction of their work.

Q. Is it easy to gain membership in one of the building trades unions?

A. No, and in spite of some modern evidence to the contrary, it is never easy to gain a worthwhile goal. Qualifications for membership in those unions are high because their standards of craftsmanship are high. Those high standards protect both the employer and the public.

Q. Do the unions obtain most new members from candidates that were recommended by relatives or friends of union members?

A. Some new members come in in that manner, and it would be rather strange if they did not. That charge may have had more validity some years ago when good jobs were limited. At present only a limited number of new members have had such sponsorship.

Q. Are the candidates who are sponsored by a relative, friends, or other union members exempt from the usual qualifications?

A. No. Such candidates are subject to the same investigation and the same examination given to other candidates.

Q. The wages and fringe benefits for building trades craftsmen are very good. Are those wage rates uniform throughout the United States and Canada?

A. No. Each area sets its own wage pattern. The rates must be competitive and are usually based on rates paid for jobs requiring equivalent skills in each area.

Q. Do some qualified men fail to apply for membership in a building trades union because they have been misinformed on the subject of qualifications for membership?

A. That could be true, but it seems more reasonable to believe that qualified men fail to apply for membership for the very simple reason that they do not know how to make the first move.

Q. When a man decides to seek membership in a building trades union, why is it important for him to be persistent?

A. Construction is a seasonal and cyclical industry, and when building activity is slow, the unions may have men on the out-of-work lists. At such times they may not encourage a candidate to apply for membership. A few months later, with construction activity more promising, a candidate would probably receive a much warmer welcome.

Q. Could the right sponsor be an important factor in gaining membership in one of those unions?

A. Yes. With all other elements equal, a good sponsor could make all the difference.

Q. Do all of the building trades unions operate in the same manner and under the same set of rules?

A. No. Wide variation is found in the operating methods of those unions. When making application for membership it would be necessary to explore the conditions and rules that exist in the area in which membership is sought.

Q. Does a candidate get just one shot at the qualifying examination?

A. No. Many men fail the examination on the first try, but when they learn what is expected of them, most get a passing grade on the second try.

Q. How does a candidate find the unions?

A. They are always listed in the telephone book or the city directory.

CHAPTER III

Unions Must Take in New Members

On January 1, 1952, the building and construction trades unions had a combined membership of approximately 3,000,000. On January 1, 1967, the combined membership of those unions was still near the 3,000,000 level. During that period the unions had to run very fast just to stand still. Not all of the unions fared the same; one or two held about even, several lost ground, but a number of the more progressive made substantial gains.

The fact that most building trades unions were unable to increase memberships over a period of fifteen years does not mean that they failed to do an effective job of organizing and training. On the contrary, the unions did a fine job, but they were the victims of long-developing combinations of circumstances over which they had little control.

Part of the problem dated back to the days of the great depression in the 1930's when very few men were trained for jobs in the construction industry, for the very good reason that no jobs were available. The situation was further aggravated during World War II when the building trades unions were forced to take in many men who were older than usual. It would be hard to estimate the ages of men who came into the unions at that time, but many of them came out of retirement and their average age was probably twenty years above normal.

All of which accounts for the fact that the unions could make no gain in membership for more than fifteen years following the Korean war. That situation may have been tough for the unions, but it has been, and will continue to be, a good break for men who seek jobs in the construction industry. It would not be possible to estimate the number of new members the unions will need to take in over the next ten years to hold present membership levels, but the figure would be high.

It is true that many older members have died or retired, which could lower replacement requirements, but a new element has been added that must be taken into consideration. Over the past ten years the building trades unions have negotiated very generous retirement and pension plans. Many members will be able to retire with a good income after twenty-five years of accrued benefits, and others may elect to retire with fewer pension credits. In addition, other union members may decide to freeze pension benefits after fifteen or twenty years and start a new career.

The exact number of members in the building trades unions in early 1970 is not known, but some authorities place the figure as high as 4,000,000. Even that high figure, however, would not include building trades craftsmen who are members of an in-plant union, nonunion, or workers who are employed on maintenance, service, repair, and operating jobs. That total might exceed 6,000,000. A conservative estimate of membership loss through death, retirement, or resignation would run from 10 to 20 percent of all construction workers.

Trying to project workers' needs for the future is a chancy business, but it would be fair to assume that every member who quits the construction industry for any cause will leave a job opening that must be filled. That means the arithmetic of building trades unions membership replacement for the next few years might be somewhat as follows:

Apprentice Openings Each Year, All Trades	125,000
Specialists, All Fields	100,000
Hod Carriers, Laborers, and Helpers	75,000
Journeymen, All Trades	200,000
Total	500,000

At best those estimates are guesses, but it is possible that they

Under the watchful eye of an inspector, journeyman mechanics install a low-pressure turbine lubrication pump and check the shaft alignment.

are much too conservative. They are based on present membership levels and do not allow for growth. Nor do they include the many employment opportunities in service, maintenance, and operating.

The man who seeks membership in a building trades union will always deal with the local union for his trade, and that can be difficult. The national unions are fully aware of the need to organize and take in new members, but many local unions do not go along with national union policy. On the contrary, many local unions seem determined to hold memberships to existing levels, or lower.

Local union members and officials do not seem to be able to grasp the fact that their union does not have the exclusive right to organize building trades workers. As a result, many skilled mechanics, especially in the newer fields, such as air conditioning and refrigeration, have had to turn to other labor organizations to find representation.

Those labor organizations that are outside the building trades may be able to give their members adequate representation in bargaining for wages and fringe benefits, but they are bound to fail in the one area that is of vital importance to every craftsman and employer in the industry, and for the consumer as well. Those outside labor organizations do not have the desire, the resources, the experience, or the know-how to train and develop the highly skilled craftsmen that are so vital to the entire construction industry.

Questions and Answers

Q. Why will it be necessary for the building trades unions to take in new members?

A. The reasons go back many years to the depression when few craftsmen were trained; was aggravated during World War II when many older men came in, and now generous pensions and early retirement will be an important factor adding to the problem.

Q. Will the loss of membership through death, retirement, and resignation continue at the present rate into the future?

A. That trend will continue for many years until enough younger men are brought in to effect a more favorable age balance.

Q. Does that situation work to the advantage of men who might want to join one of the building trades unions?

A. Yes. The unions must continue their efforts to organize and expand memberships, or lose out to more aggressive labor organizations.

Q. Do the building trades unions have the exclusive right to organize the craftsmen of the construction industry?

A. They do not. No labor organization has the exclusive right to organize the industry.

Q. How do the unions decide on the number of apprentice members to be taken in each year?

A. That is determined on a percentage basis. Many building trades unions will allow up to one apprentice for each five journeymen.

Q. Would it be possible for the building trades unions to freeze memberships at present levels?

A. No. That would not work. Loss by death and retirement would soon decimate the ranks of any labor organization that took such action.

Q. When the unions take in apprentice members do the journeyman members feel that those apprentices are in competition for existing jobs?

A. Not as a rule. The ratio of apprentices to journeymen is the one factor in union membership that remains fairly constant. In most instances, local unions will bring in only enough apprentice members to replace those who have graduated to journeyman, or quit the trade.

Q. The building trades unions take in many men on the journeyman level. If these men did not serve an apprenticeship with the union, how can they qualify for membership?

A. Many of those men may have completed an informal apprenticeship that included work experience gained while working in nonunion shops, industrial plants, civil service, or on maintenance and repair work in areas that had no union for them to join.

Q. Why would men want to leave such jobs to become members of a building trades union?

A. That is easy to explain. Those men are attracted by the good wages, fringe benefits, and superior working conditions that are available in the mainstream of construction.

Q. Do the building trades unions maintain higher standards of craftsmanship than other occupational fields in which similar skills are required?

A. Yes. There can be no question about that. Those unions have had much experience in training craftsmen for the building trades and they do a good job.

Q. Could an outside labor organization equal such training for building trades craftsmen?

A. It is not likely they would make the effort.

Q. Is there one single factor that might affect the conditions for membership in building trades unions?

A. The single factor that could affect such conditions might lie in the fact that the sons of members may not be so quick to follow in father's footsteps. Many of those young men have the desire and the resources to complete a college education. With that level of education completed, many careers will be open.

CHAPTER IV

The Building and Construction Trades Unions

Very few people, including many of the men who work in the building trades, have a clear understanding of the good jobs and fine opportunities for advancement that are available in the construction industry. Most construction trades have several branches and a number of specialties, and the apprentice and journeyman-training programs are designed to give a craftsman a very broad education in every phase of his craft. Unfortunately, many men who start such training often decide to be satisfied with one of the special work activities. A special skill of that sort is very limiting, and often the field is overcrowded. If men who are entering those trades could be made aware of all that they have to offer, they might make a wiser choice.

The following pages give a brief outline of the job opportunities available in several of the largest building trades unions. The unions were selected for outline because their field of operation is so large and so diversified that many of their activities are not known to the uninitiated.

It should be understood that the jurisdiction of work that is set out for each union will vary somewhat from one section of the country to another, and that a certain amount of overlapping will occur in jurisdictional matters. Many of those work jurisdictions go back several years and they were not always made along strictly craft lines. As industry developed in the United States and moved away from the older centers of population,

35

work assignments were often made to whatever labor organization happened to be in control at that moment.

Later, as new industrial areas developed, the building trades unions moved in and set up shop, laying claim to all work assignments they considered to be theirs. In many instances, if the existing work assignments had been in existence for some time, they were allowed to stand. In other instances changes were made.

The old precedents, which set the pattern for many older work assignments, have been the source of many a squabble between labor organizations. The average person, who could not expect to be informed on such matters, is often annoyed by such interunion quarrels. The inconvenience might be easier to bear if the individual could be made to understand that all labor unions are convinced they are fighting to protect what is rightfully theirs.

The Boilermakers Union (*150,000 members*)

It would be a mistake to believe that the work of the boilermaker is confined to the erection of steam boilers, steam pressure vessels, and certain heat exchangers. In reality, this trade has several branches and a number of specialties. These craftsmen are responsible for the fabrication and erection of every type of pressure vessel used in oil refining, chemical processing, and such. They also fabricate and erect many types of bolted, riveted, and welded tanks. Much of that work must be done to the most exacting specifications. Special skills for boilermakers include welding, chipping, rigging, burning, layout, and many others.

The boilermakers also have a very wide jurisdiction in the shipbuilding industry, in which they are responsible for fabrication of hull components, framing of the hull, installation of hull plates, and the like. This branch of the trade offers jobs for men who are skilled in rigging, welding, burning, grinding, chipping, riveting, shrinking, pattern making, layout, etc. All of those jobs command a good wage, fringe benefits, and fine working conditions.

The Carpenters and Joiners Union (860,000 members)

This is another union that offers a wide variety of jobs, requiring many degrees of skill. A carpenter may be required to build any structure made of wood, from a rough temporary bridge to the finest cabinet work. Carpenters build the forms for concrete construction, erect the framing of all wood structure buildings, put down all sheathing and subflooring, set all window frames, hang all doors, install locks and hardware and related trim, and many other jobs.

In some areas the carpenters have jurisdiction over the millrights. Millrights install much of the equipment in factories, warehouses, packing sheds, oil refineries, chemical plants, etc. The carpenters also have quite a broad jurisdiction of work in shipbuilding. Although most ships are now built of steel, carpenters are needed to install boat cradles, launching devices, handrails, decks, cargo gratings, and such.

In addition, carpenters are responsible for building scaffolding, temporary ladders, working platforms, and other structures. One branch of the carpenters trade is responsible for building docks, piers, and shipbuilding ways. They must also prepare the ways for launching a ship. All are fine jobs, at good pay and with excellent working conditions.

The Electrical Workers Union (I.B.E.W.)
(800,000 members)

The jurisdiction of work for the electrician is probably the most diversified of all the building and construction trades. Jobs are available in this field for men with every degree of skill from a specialist in the bending and installation of conduit piping to the man with a degree in electrical engineering. These

In a central control room, with all wiring, instruments, and electrical devices installed, mechanics check out the circuits and test the operation.

craftsmen install and service every type of electrical device from a fractional horsepower electric motor to a huge generator that can deliver thousands of units of electrical energy.

All of the jobs mentioned above—and dozens of other skills—are duplicated in the shipbuilding industry. The man who selects the electrical craft for a lifetime vocation will never have to put a limit on his ambition. Craft skills on the journeyman level are unlimited, and supervisory jobs range from that of foreman over a small crew on a commercial or light industrial building project to that of superintendent on a huge construction project employing hundreds of electricians.

Laborers and Hod Carriers (476,000 members)

At one time the hod carrier was thought to be a worker who carried trays of bricks and mortar on his shoulder, but this image is no longer true. Today the hod carrier, or tender, is a man whose work calls for a much higher degree of skill and experience. The tender still handles brick and mortar, but he is seldom required to carry the materials on his shoulder.

Most mortar and plaster is now delivered to the job in a premixed state and requires only the addition of water to make it usable. A special machine mixes the plaster and pumps it to any location in the building through flexible tubing. Bricks, building blocks, and other material are moved to working locations by portable hoists or elevators. Modern bricklayers or masons seldom cut a brick or block to size on the work platform. They give the correct dimensions to the tender, who then cuts the material to size with a power saw or other cutting device.

Building laborers share the same union with the hod carriers. In the past a building or common laborer was a man who dug ditches for sewer lines, did excavating for foundations, and cleaned up trash and scrap material on the construction site. The laborers still perform those important tasks, but most of the digging and excavating is now done by machines.

The modern building laborer must learn to operate many types of pneumatic equipment, including jackhammers, drills, impact tools, vibrators, and pumps. The laborer is often assigned to work as a helper with the carpenters, cement finishers, and other craftsmen. On highway construction the laborer acts as flagman and traffic control man. In fact, much of the work activity of the building laborer calls for a degree of skill equivalent to the specialist in many trades. In recent years these men have been given the recognition that is their due, and pay rates and fringe benefits are very good. The know-how for the jobs is acquired by on-the-job work experience.

Bridge and Structural Ironworkers (146,000 members)

The craftsmen of this trade are responsible for the erection of structural steel building frames, radio towers, bridges, and all other building projects in which structural steel fabrications are used. The trade also has many special branches, such as welding, riveting, burning, chipping, and rigging. The ironworker must be able to read blueprints or working drawings and he must learn the various codes used in marking materials and structural shapes for identification. The fabrications for any structure are shop-fabricated and every item must be marked for identification. On a large structure thousands of such items, large and small, may be used. To unload, segregate, and stockpile such material for easy accessibility is one of the most important skills the ironworker must master.

A certain percentage of all ironworkers will be required to "go high" on steel structures as the framework of the building rises, but not all ironworkers engage in high climbing. On the contrary, for every man who works high on steel structure erection, ten additional ironworkers may be working at ground level, or on work platforms reached by stairways or ladders. Much of that work is on the installation of handrails, guard rails, floor plates, steel ladders, platforms, and catwalks. The ironworker is also required to operate a wide variety of power equipment.

Another, very important, branch of the ironworker's trade is the job of installing reinforcing bars or material in the forms before concrete is poured. These ironworkers (sometimes called rod-busters) are responsible for placing all re-bar or other reinforcing material in place. Such material must be installed to exact specifications for size, weight, and shape. The working drawings used by the rod-buster are among the most complex in the construction industry. In some instances the ironworker may be required to draw his own working sketches. The job of the rod-buster does not have the spectacular quality of the high-climbing steel erector, but it is a fine skill and of the utmost importance on every construction job in which steel and concrete are used.

The Pipefitting Industry (285,000 members)

The pipe trades are among the oldest and most diversified in the building and construction industry, with many branch trades and special skills. Plumbing is probably the oldest branch of the trade, and the work is so well known that no outline is necessary. It should be noted, however, that proficiency in plumbing skills can lead to such jobs as foreman, estimator, mechanical drawing detailer, inspector, trade school instructor, or to master plumber and the ownership of a contracting business.

Pipefitter/Steamfitter

The mechanics of these trades work on every type of construction project, but the greatest number are employed on the installation and maintenance of piping systems and components for oil refineries, chemical plants, atomic energy plants, electric power plants, missile bases, dams, factories, and the like.

In many respects these jobs are the most fascinating of all in the industry. Pipefitter/steamfitters are employed by the large national and international piping contractors on construction projects in many parts of the world. Most employment is on larger building projects, and few activities can equal the excitement and satisfaction that comes with being a part of the crew on a huge building operation as it shapes up through the various stages of construction.

Refrigeration and Air Conditioning

In a sense this is the baby of the pipe trades, and possibly the least understood of any of the building trades. Men from all walks of life read of new developments in the field and are drawn to it in the belief that they will find a worthwhile vocation. Some fine job opportunities are available in air conditioning and refrigeration, and the field has many specialized branches. Unfortunately, however, all too few men ever really master the trade or the group of related work activities. Many men stay with a training program until they learn enough just to get by at one of the specialties and are thus doomed to remain in that limited field of operation. That is a mistake. The best jobs in air conditioning and refrigeration go to the mechanics with the best background of technical education and on-the-job work experience.

(*Note:* Many authorities are convinced that the combined fields of air conditioning and refrigeration sales, installation, service, maintenance, and operation will grow to be the largest single job opportunity field in the pipe trades.)

Metal Trades Branches of the Pipe Trades

The metal trades are not as well known as some other branches of the pipe trades, partly because many local unions for the pipe trades do not have a metal trades division. That does not mean metal trades jobs are less important than other branches, or less desirable as a vocational activity. Metal trades job openings are to be found in shipbuilding and ship repair, manufacturing of pumps, air compressors, instrument panels, and other units in which pipe fittings and components are installed at the factory and shipped as units.

Shipbuilding, ship conversion, and ship repair offer fine jobs for many metal trades craftsmen. Miles and miles of nearly every type of pipe and tubing are used in every ship, and every inch of those installations is a challenge. Space is at a premium on all ships, and the routing, installation, and protection of piping and components often require great ingenuity and skill. It is a fine career field for men who live in shipbuilding areas.

Miscellaneous Branches of the Pipe Trades

In addition to the main branches of the pipe trades outlined above, there are a number of specialized branches of the pipe trades that are not so well known, but that offer some fine career opportunities. They include sprinkler fitter, coppersmith, hydraulic fitter, railroad fitter, instrument fitter, and a number of others.

One quite large field of opportunity for men who have mastered pipe trades skills is civil service—city, county, state, or federal. Much of the work falls under the classifications of service, repair, maintenance, and operation, but certain naval shipyards, missile bases, and other defense installations offer the full range of new construction jobs.

One little-known aspect of holding a journeyman card in a building and construction trades union, or other agency by which certificates of proficiency are issued, is the unexpected bonus involved. In many instances the presentation of a paid-up union card on the journeyman level, or a certificate of proficiency, is all that is required to convince employers that a craftsman is qualified. In addition, a paid-up union card can be an excellent character reference. The completion of an apprenticeship and graduation to journeyman is pretty convincing evidence that the individual has been willing and able to accept the discipline of extended education and training.

Welding

Welding is considered to be a tool of every trade, and the

A welder and a machinist install blades on a low-pressure turbine rotor.

welders who work in the construction industry do not have their own union. Each craft develops its own welders, with the special skills required for that trade. In the construction field not much welding can be classed as production work, that is, a job in which a man does nothing but welding. The welders of the building trades are not limited to welding, but are required to have related skills that will put them on an equal footing with all journeymen in the industry. The welder has every opportunity to advance to foreman, layout man, fabrication specialist, and many other jobs. Because welding is a tool of every building trade that involves metal, skill in the craft is often used as a means to gain entry into a specialty union.

Operating Engineers (285,000 members)

The operating engineers in the building trades are responsible for repairs and operation of all construction equipment, such as truck cranes, stiff-leg cranes, gantry cranes, draglines, gas shovels, and road-building equipment. Members include operators, oilers, helpers, heavy-duty mechanics, among others.

Bricklayers, Masons, and Plasterers (158,000 members)

Members of the Bricklayers, Masons and Plasterers International Union of America are responsible for laying brick, cement blocks, tile, and other materials used for building walls, partitions, gardens, etc. The work includes much decorative installations for fireplaces, special effects, and stone installations. The work of the plasterer is too well known to need outlining, but that field, too, has much work that requires skill in decorative and special effects.

Painters and Paperhangers (201,000 members)

The jurisdiction of the Brotherhood of Painters, Paperhangers and Decorators of America is well known and needs no outline. It might be thought that such work is on the decline because so many homeowners go in for do-it-yourself painting, but that is only one phase of the painters' work. Commercial and industrial jobs account for a far greater percentage of work in the industry. In addition, for a really professional job of painting or paperhanging, the homeowner must turn to the professionals who have the skill. The field offers fine job opportunities.

Sheet Metal Workers (85,000 members)

The Sheet Metal Workers International Union has always had a wide jurisdiction in heating, cooling, ventilation, and roofing, as well as special work in the fabrication of ventilation hoods for kitchens, commercial, and industrial installation. Now, with the growth of air conditioning, the union is moving into air-conditioning installation and service work. It is a fine skill, in an expanding field.

The following trades and special skills are considered part of the building and construction trades. Some of them have their own separate union. Others are considered specialties of another trade. Jurisdiction over such work varies from one section to another. Specific information should be obtained in each area.

Carpet and Soft Tile Layers   *Pipe, Boiler and Pressure*
Cement Finishers   *Vessel-Insulators*
Elevator Installers   *Roofers*
Fixture and Showcase Installers *Scaffold Erectors*
Glaziers   *Seating Installers*
Lathers   *Tilesetters*
                                  Vessel Insulation

(*Note:* Certain other labor unions, such as the teamsters and machinists, have many members who work on building and construction projects, but those unions are not classified with the building trades under normal conditions.

Questions and Answers

Q. Is the above list of building and construction trades unions complete?

A. No. Only those with the largest memberships have been outlined.

Q. Do the building and construction trades unions control all the jobs in the industry?

A. No. Quite a segment of all building is done by nonunion mechanics, or by members of an in-plant union. That is especially true of revision, expansion, and changes in an existing plant. In addition, much maintenance and service work is done by mechanics who have never been organized.

Q. Are most jurisdictional disputes that involve unions of the construction industry caused by an attempt to grab power and additional jurisdiction?

A. No, this is seldom true in the building trades. The number of jobs involved in any single dispute would not justify a strike. In many instances jurisdictional disputes involve some matter of principle, with both sides fighting to protect and hold what they believe to be rightfully theirs.

Q. Why are the welders who work in the building trades denied the right to have their own union?

A. "Denied the right" is hardly the proper term. Welding is a comparative latecomer to the building trades and has always been considered to be a tool of every trade.

Q. Is this fair to the welder?

A. Yes, it is a fair arrangement. The welders who work with each craft are not limited to welding. They have every opportunity to advance to jobs of broader scope. The only limiting factor is the ambition of the individual.

Q. In the outlines for a number of the building trades unions, certain specialties are mentioned. Does a mechanic have to serve a five-year apprenticeship to master one of the those specialties?

A. No, but it would be wise to serve a full apprenticeship before selecting a specialty. Advancement opportunities for the specialist are limited. The fully qualified journeyman mechanic will have a much larger field to operate in, with almost unlimited chance for advancement.

Q. Does a man have to serve a four- or five-year apprenticeship to become a building laborer, scaffold erector, seating installer, etc.?

A. No. The skill and experience for such jobs are gained while working as a helper. However, the candidate for a job in the construction industry should always be aware of one fact: Any job that can be mastered in a short time does not offer the same chances for advancement that are open to a fully qualified journeyman mechanic.

Q. Do jobs in the building trades offer chances for advancement?

A. Yes. Few occupational fields offer equal career advancement opportunities.

Q. Would it be wise for an apprentice to specialize in one of the limited branches of his trade?

A. No. Every apprentice should strive to gain the widest possible experience in his trade. With a good background of training and experience it is much easier to select the special trade skills that are suited to the individual's ability, temperament, and the job opportunities available in his area.

Q. Employers in the building trades may range from a local contractor who employs only one or two mechanics, to an industrial piping contractor who operates worldwide. Which type of employer should the apprentice choose?

A. The apprentice will be confined, in most instances, to the employers who operate in his home locality, or to contractors who come into the area to erect building projects for which they have bid.

Q. Does that mean the apprentice cannot transfer to another local union for his trade, or that he cannot travel to construction jobs in other areas for his own convenience?

A. It is generally expected that the apprentice will stay within the territory of the local union that indentured him as an apprentice in the trade until he graduates to journeyman. There are exceptions, but that is a question that could be answered only when, and if, it comes up.

Q. What would be the advantages of working for one of the big national or international construction companies?

A. Such jobs might mean a chance to travel; a wider choice of work assignments; better chance for advancement; and the fact that the employee is not required to deal directly with the public.

Q. What would be the advantage of a job in maintenance and repair work for the building trades journeyman?

A. Such a job might mean steady work in the same shop year after year. Transportation might be less of a problem and certain benefits are to be gained by staying under the health, welfare, pension plans, etc., of a single employer.

Q. What special advantages are to be found in jobs that involve air conditioning and refrigeration?

A. The field offers a wide variety of fascinating work, but in the building trades unions such work is limited to a few crafts, such as pipefitters, sheet metal workers, machinists, etc.

Q. Is the construction industry a growth field?

A. Yes, job opportunities in the building trades are expanding, and the skill requirements for those trades grow more sophisticated each year.

Q. What special advantages does the welding trade offer?

A. Welding has never been classed as a separate trade in the building industry, but is an essential part of nearly all construction crafts. The welder has the same chance for advancement as other journeymen in each trade.

Q. Is the building trades mechanic who is a member of a labor union free to start his own contracting business?

A. Yes, many building trades journeymen mechanics go on to qualify as master mechanics and establish a successful contracting business.

Q. What advancement opportunities might be open to the building trades mechanic who has worked at his trade for a few years?

A. Such men might be offered jobs as foreman, general foreman, inspector, instructor, estimator, salesman, etc.

Q. Are those advancement opportunities few and far between?

A. No. On the contrary, one of the greatest problems of building trades employers is to find enough qualified mechanics who have the ability, and who are willing, to assume greater responsibility.

Q. How can a paid-up union card in one of the building trades unions help a man to get a better job?

A. In many instances a paid-up union card is all that is needed to prove that a man is qualified to work at his trade. That form of evidence is accepted for many civil service jobs, and for jobs in private industry in which an employer is not affiliated with a labor union.

Q. Why is such evidence accepted?
A. The fact that a man has successfully completed an apprenticeship and graduated to the journeyman level indicates that he has the ability to accept discipline.

Q. Would that be the only criterion by which the employer would be guided?
A. Certainly not. Most employers would carry out an investigation with regard to ability, stability of character, general attitude, etc. In addition, many construction projects require some form of security clearance. To work on such jobs a man must have a clear record, or be able to show that he is reliable.

Q. What are the advantages of a job in civil service for a building trades trainee or journeyman?
A. Many civil service jobs offer steady work at good pay and good fringe benefits.

Q. Is there much movement by building trades mechanics from the construction industry to civil service jobs?
A. There is always some change, and the movement is both ways. Men move from construction to civil service at the same time that men are moving from civil service into construction.

Q. Why does that happen?
A. There are many reasons. Ambitious men who have jobs in

civil service may feel they will find a better way of life in the mainstream of the construction industry, where the action is. Men who hold jobs in the construction industry may want to move into a somewhat less competitive atmosphere.

CHAPTER V

Apprentice Selection and Training

The ideal way for any building trades union to maintain a desirable level of membership is by way of an apprentice-training program. Under such conditions men come into the union at an age when they are more adaptable, more flexible in attitudes, and more willing to accept the discipline of an extended training program. The unions could be more selective and they could require every candidate for an apprenticeship to have a high-school education, and tests could be given to determine the fitness of any man to enter a trade in the field.

In the past there have usually been far more applicants for every apprenticeship than there were openings in the programs. That situation is changing as new job opportunity fields open up, and a few unions have had to make an effort to recruit men to fill the jobs. When men are recruited on the open labor market, candidates are required to pass an examination similar to those used to determine ability and fitness for equivalent jobs in business, industry, or civil service.

Such an examination, and the study needed to prepare for it, might give the candidates a better understanding of the field, and the responsibility required by membership in one of the building trades unions. When a young man is accepted as an apprentice in the building trades he is given the opportunity to qualify for an excellent career. An apprenticeship is a valuable property and should be treated as such. To illustrate the value of an apprenticeship the candidate should consider these facts: In many occupations a student-trainee is required to attend school for several years, entirely at his own expense. He may then be required to work at low pay for several more years to qualify for a responsible job. Many student-trainees, even if they do complete their training and internship, may never achieve an income level equivalent to a journeyman mechanic in the building trades.

The building trades apprentice receives a very good wage from his first day on the job, plus automatic raises for each period of training completed. He also receives all fringe benefits that are paid to journeyman mechanics of his trade, and all the protection of his rights that union membership brings.

Wages for building trades mechanics vary from one area to another, but at the start of 1970 the average wage for all journeymen and specialists in the field was a minimum of $5.50 per hour. (In late 1969 statistics released by the U.S. Department of Labor set the average wage for all building trades journeymen at $5.57 per hour. Fringe benefits added another 50¢ per hour.)

For the sake of simplicity the wage rate for the following table of pay rates for apprentices has been set at $5.50 per hour. (It should be understood that these are average figures. In some areas rates may be lower; in other areas they may be substantially higher.)

(*Note:* The first six-month period is probationary. The apprentice is not inducted into the union until he has completed such probation and achieved a satisfactory grade. In a sense that gives both the union and the probationer a second choice.)

1st six-month period			50 percent of journeyman rate				$2.75 per hour		
2nd "	"	"	55	"	"	"	"	3.02½	"	"
3rd "	"	"	60	"	"	"	"	3.30	"	"
4th "	"	"	65	"	"	"	"	3.57½	"	"
5th "	"	"	70	"	"	"	"	3.85	"	"
6th "	"	"	75	"	"	"	"	4.12½	"	"
7th "	"	"	80	"	"	"	"	4.40	"	"
8th "	"	"	85	"	"	"	"	4.67½	"	"
9th "	"	"	90	"	"	"	"	4.95	"	"
10th "	"	"	95	"	"	"	"	5.22½	"	"

At the end of the tenth six-month period the apprentice who has completed the training to the satisfaction of the Joint Apprenticeship Committee will be graduated to journeyman mechanic. It is worth repeating that the apprentice will receive all fringe benefits paid to journeymen. That should add another 10 percent to his wages.

All apprentice-training programs for the building trades unions must meet minimum state and federal rules and regulations. (The training programs for most building trades unions exceed the minimum by a substantial margin.)

The building trades unions have every right, and the duty, to select the best men available to fill vacancies in the ranks of apprentices, and there should be no complaints on that score. Any candidate who doubts the value of an apprenticeship would be wise to compare the wages, fringe benefits, working conditions, and general career opportunity with the vocational opportunities that might be open to him in other fields.

Discipline is essential in any school or training program that is to last for any length of time. Some discipline will be imposed by instructors in the classroom and by the Joint Apprenticeship Committee, but much of the discipline must be self-imposed. Most apprentices recognize the need for discipline in the program and on the job, but there may be some difference of opinion as to what constitutes fair, but adequate, discipline. To state it briefly, discipline in an apprentice-training program means the acceptance of rules that will ensure an orderly progression throughout the entire training program. If discipline breaks down the program cannot be effective. The ability to apply self-discipline to any personal effort is the mark of the mature individual.

The apprentice-training programs for the building trades are the responsibility of the Joint Apprenticeship Committee that is made up of an equal number of men from the employers and the union. The committee has the power to discipline an apprentice, and the discipline could range from a warning to a setback of one

Electricians installing a 500,000-volt circuit breaker at a powerhouse switchyard.

or more periods, or even removal from the program. When an apprentice is removed by action of the committee, he is automatically dropped from the union. If an apprentice is set back for one or more periods, or fails to advance to the next period, periodic raises are delayed. The apprentice must earn his advancement by his effort in the classroom and his work on the job.

Many of the instructors in the apprentice-training programs are mechanics who are working at the trade they teach. Those men are well trained and devoted to the task of training. The instructor is paid for the time he spends in the classroom, but that is only part of the teaching job. Additional work includes the preparation of lessons, tests, grading of test papers, and meetings with the Joint Apprenticeship Committee. The instructor must also work with employers and the business manager of the local union to protect the interests of the apprentice. He must try to meet the needs of each apprentice in his class and the class as a whole.

In an apprenticeship, as in any other important course of action, men get out of the program only as much as they are willing to put into it. If an apprentice makes a feeble and half-hearted effort, he will reap a feeble reward. A careless, lazy, and indifferent apprentice will, if he does manage to hang on and graduate to journeyman mechanic, be a careless, lazy, and indifferent craftsman. Such individuals are not much in demand. They are avoided by employers and held in contempt by fellow employees.

The apprentice-training programs have all of the elements needed to develop qualified craftsmen, and a sincere effort during the apprenticeship can lay the foundation for a lifetime of rewarding activity. An apprenticeship is an investment in the future. It may be the most important investment a man will ever make.

Questions and Answers

Q. How can an apprentice be sure he has chosen the right vocation?

A. There is no sure way, but pre-entry examinations and aptitude tests are valuable aids. In addition, in most apprentice-training programs candidates are required to serve a probationary period of six months. After six months of on-the-job work experience and classroom attendance, the decision whether to quit or continue should not be too difficult to make.

Q. Is the attitude an apprentice may have toward labor unions in general, and the union he will be required to join, important to the apprentice?

A. Yes, such attitudes are very important, and the apprentice should have no mental reservations. If a man is disturbed by the idea of becoming a member of a labor union, he should select a vocation in which such membership is not required.

Q. Most apprentices start their training with little past work experience. Does that mean they will be assigned to such tasks as cleaning the shop, moving material, and other dirty jobs?

A. Every apprentice will draw some tasks of the sort, as the journeyman mechanics do, but most job assignments will be on work that is related to the trade.

Q. Is an apprentice-training program a good way to master one of the building and construction trades?

A. Yes, it is the very best way. It has been proven that no better method exists for training craftsmen than by on-the-job work experience and classroom educational effort.

Q. Do the local unions of the building trades have the right to be selective as to men they accept into their apprentice-training programs?

A. They not only have the right, they have a duty to seek out the men with the highest potential.

Q. Will the apprentice be expected to accept the discipline that goes with every training program?

A. Yes. The apprentice is expected to give a fair day's work for each day he is paid, attend the required classes, and maintain a high interest level at all times. He should have respect for his employer, his foreman, instructors, and fellow workers.

Q. What happens if the apprentice has an indifferent attitude toward his job, fails to attend classes, and fails to generate a reasonable level of interest in mastering his trade?

A. He could be warned, reprimanded, set back in the program, or dropped from the apprentice program and the union.

Q. Does the local union have sole responsibility for administering the apprentice-training program?

A. No. It is a joint effort of management and labor. The Joint Apprenticeship Committee of the local union is made up of an equal number of members from the employers and union members.

Q. Does an apprentice in the building trades start at a very low wage?

A. No. The apprentice starts at a very good wage and receives periodic raises at regular intervals throughout the apprenticeship—usually each six months, if his record is satisfactory.

Q. Are the apprentice-training programs effective and efficient?

A. Yes. They are fine programs and are under constant review. Every effort is made to improve the training and have it reflect changing conditions and new developments.

Q. Who does the teaching in the apprentice-training programs?

A. In most instances the instructor will be a member of the union for his trade.

Q. Is the instructor well paid for his work?

A. The instructor is paid for the time he spends in the classroom. He is not paid for extra work, counseling time, etc.

Q. Why do instructors take on the responsibility of such jobs?

A. Instructors have been known to ask themselves that question. To most men it is their contribution to the community, their local union, and good craftsmanship.

Q. What happens if an apprentice does not take an interest in his work or classroom training?

A. Competition is keen and will become increasingly so as more young men become aware of the fine opportunity offered by an apprenticeship. An apprentice who fails to give his best effort may be dropped from the program.

Q. What will be the result if the apprentice applies his best effort to his job and training program?

A. By the time such a man graduates to journeyman his reputation will be well established. He will be respected by employers and fellow workers. His services will be in demand.

Q. Are wage rates for building trades craftsmen uniform in all sections of the United States?

A. No. There is quite a wide variation in wage rates and fringe benefits paid. Such rates are usually based on wages paid for jobs of equivalent skill in each area.

Q. When local unions openly recruit candidates to enter an apprenticeship in the building trades, are men accepted on a first-come basis?

A. No. All candidates are subject to aptitude tests and other qualification measures.

CHAPTER VI

How an Apprentice Masters His Trade

Nothing is easy about mastering one of the building and construction trades. The long-range project takes dedication and hard work, but those factors are all to the good. If the trades were easy to learn, every craft would be flooded with would-be mechanics.

When a young man starts a course of education and training that will take several years to complete, the road ahead seems very long. Fortunately, learning a trade is a gradual process, and in most instances the apprentice is making greater progress than seems apparent in the early stages, and he receives a good rate of pay for his effort.

Much of what the apprentice has to learn will be taught in the classroom and through on-the-job work activity, but a great deal of knowledge will come by indirection. As he works and studies, the apprentice gradually absorbs the fundamentals of his trade. Once a sound foundation of fundamentals has been laid, learning is easier and progress is faster.

Progress in learning a trade could be speeded up if the apprentice would approach the fundamentals with system and order. The first step in an orderly progression might be for the apprentice to make up an outline of those things that are basic to the craft he seeks to master. That list should include many of the things an apprentice will be expected to know from his first day on the job. He could then concentrate on those basic requirements. The list would not be too long, and one thing would, inevitably, lead to another.

In every building and construction trade there is a great need

61

to develop skill in taking measurements. In many instances it takes two men to measure work to be fabricated and installed, and each man must understand what the other is doing at all times. In fact, the taking of field measurements during the early days of a construction project is an art that cannot be mastered quickly. The craftsman must learn to read a folding rule, or tapeline, with speed and accuracy, but he will not be limited to those measuring devices. He must learn to use such tools as a chalkline, plumb bob, spirit level, carpenter's square, and straight-edge.

At times it will be possible to take measurements from the working drawings for the job, but a mechanic must understand about bench marks, match lines, building lines, property lines, and other reference marks. He must understand what is meant by "grade" for each job; how "grade" is determined, and how to figure plus or minus elevations from "grade." The apprentice will not be expected to be master of those things in the early days of his apprenticeship, but he should be on notice as to their importance.

Along with the taking of field measurements, and of equal importance, is the ability to work simple arithmetic problems quickly and accurately. A working knowledge of arithmetic, fractions, decimals, and the use of a few constants that are used to figure offsets, areas of circles, capacity of tanks, area of surfaces, etc., is essential.

Possibly the second most important fundamental the apprentice should learn is the recognition and identity of fittings, fixtures, materials, and special tools used in his trade. Every craftsman in the building trades will have occasion to use an almost unbelievable variety of material, and it takes time to acquire the knowledge, but a start should be made on fitting and material identification from the first day at work. One good way to acquire such knowledge is to study the catalogues of materials for the trade. They contain descriptions, photographs, diagrams, and specifications. A few hours each week spent in poring over such a catalogue will pay big dividends.

In instances in which welding is a tool of the trade, it is a good idea for the apprentice to learn to identify the size and type of welding rods in common use. That should include information on soldering alloys, silver solder alloys, cleaning compounds, methods used in soldering, type of flux used, and so on. For his own protection, and for the protection of the men he works with, the apprentice should learn something about the dangers in the use of such items as common cleaning solvents, cleaning compounds, acids, and caustics. He should understand something of the characteristics of the bottled gases used for welding and soldering, and how these gases may react under extremes of temperature or pressure.

Every apprentice will be required to operate a wide variety of power tools, such as pipe-threading machines, power hacksaws, power drive-heads, air or electric-driven drills, grinders, impact wrenches, and many others. In addition, he will have to learn to identify and use a wide variety of hand tools. He must develop some skill in erecting scaffolding and work platforms, using extension ladders and stepladders, tying a few simple knots in rope, doing a little rigging, etc. Above all, the apprentice must learn to perform all of his work activities with his own safety, and that of his fellow workers, in mind.

Many of the above things will be taught in the classroom, whereas others will be picked up during the course of regular job assignments. The apprentice will always work under the supervision of a journeyman mechanic, and he should learn to observe and to ask pertinent questions.

One tendency of apprentices should be avoided at all costs— when an apprentice has worked in a shop that does a limited class of work for a year or two, he can get to be pretty good at his job. When that happens the apprentice may come to believe he knows enough, that more training would be a waste of time.

Ironworkers install **reinforcing** *material in the foundation for a power-house. The concrete* **forms** *are set by carpenters, and plumbers and pipe-fitters install the piping.*

That is a very foolish attitude. The apprentice who stops learning at that stage of his development will never become a fully qualified mechanic. He will be a mere specialist, with a very limited field of operation. Earnings and advancement opportunities will be equivalent to his training, experience, and skill. Any man who expects to spend many years working at any occupation would be very foolish to limit himself in such a manner.

On-the-job work activities and classroom studies are a very important part of every apprenticeship, but there are other effective methods of acquiring knowledge of a trade. Much can be learned by watching a good craftsman at work, with special attention to his overall methods of operation and his approach to any given task.

A smart mechanic will never accept a job assignment until he has all necessary information about the job. He will always get the exact location of the job, plans and specifications, tools, equipment, and materials that will be needed. In other words, he will take nothing for granted.

Many elements are involved in apprentice training and none is more important than the development of good work habits. It has been said that habit can be a slave, or it can be a master. The choice is up to the individual. The best way to avoid bad work habits is by never allowing them to take root. It takes no more time to do a job right; in fact, there is much evidence to prove that it takes less time. Careless work means careless thinking. Careless thinking can lead to time-consuming and embarrassing mistakes.

Questions and Answers

Q. Is there any quick and easy way to master one of the building trades?

A. No, fortunately. Few worthwhile careers come easily. The more difficult the field to master, the less competition there will be.

Q. What might be the most important element in learning a trade?
A. The answer to that question would, of course, be attitudes. Keen interest and dedicated application and effort are essentials in the mastery of any skilled occupation.

Q. What are some of the fundamentals the apprentice should concentrate on during the early stages of his training?
A. The fundamentals would vary with the craft, but for most trades the ability to take accurate measurements, identify a large number of fittings, fixtures, materials, special tools, etc., are of the utmost importance. Of equal importance is the question of safety.

Q. What is meant by "grade" on a construction job or building project?
A. In order to have a point of reference for vertical height of a structure, engineers must establish a "grade" for each construction job. With grade set at 0.00 for the ground-floor level, any elevation above the ground floor reads plus. Any elevation below the ground floor reads minus.

Q. What should be the attitude of the apprentice when he is required to use power tools?
A. He should have respect for those often costly tools. Read directions before using; ask questions if necessary, and make use of all required safety devices, guards, etc. He should never use a power tool that is in bad order.

Q. Can the apprentice expect to learn more in the classroom than in on-the-job work activities?
A. The apprentice will spend far more time on the job than he will in the classroom. The training programs are designed to get the most out of both methods of training.

Q. When an apprentice has worked at the trade long enough to become pretty good at certain special work, should he quit the training program and stop trying to learn?

A. No. Many apprentices are tempted to take such action, but it is always a grave mistake.

Q. Is it possible for an apprentice to learn about his trade by watching other craftsmen at work, and by asking questions?

A. Much can be learned by such methods, but the apprentice should know one thing—few craftsmen have the knack for passing on their knowledge and experience.

Q. When an apprentice is given a job assignment, what information should he demand?

A. He should get all of the information needed to do a good job. He should take nothing for granted.

Q. Does advance planning help to get a job done more efficiently?

A. Yes, advance planning is very important. When assigned to a job, one should determine what will be needed in the way of tools, materials, and transportation. He should check any plans and specifications very carefully.

Q. Why is it so important to form good work habits?

A. If bad work habits are allowed to take root, the individual will find embarrassing mistakes repeated and multiplied.

Q. How are good work habits formed?

A. By not allowing bad work habits to form.

Q. What attitude should an apprentice take when he is assigned to work with a journeyman who is obviously not qualified?

A. That could happen, but probably not as often as many apprentices would like to think. The journeyman is the senior and is responsible for the work. Let the employer be the judge of his competence.

Q. Is there much friction between apprentices and journeymen?
A. Very little, though personality clashes do occur. Sometimes apprentices in their last periods of training get to be a little too ambitious. That is considered a good sign, if not carried to extremes.

CHAPTER VII

Safety

Construction industry jobs are not considered especially hazardous, but every man who works in the building trades should be aware that some danger does exist in every occupation. From his first day on the job the apprentice will be exposed to a barrage of safety messages and safe-working bulletins, all of which are designed to put him on guard. If the apprentice does not heed such bulletins and take a sensible attitude toward safety instructions, all of the effort will be wasted.

The attitudes of employers on the subject of safe working conditions for employees will vary widely. Many employers feel they have met their responsibility if they keep their insurance paid up and abide by minimum provisions of safety laws and regulations. They seem to believe that the responsibility for working safely is a problem for the individual worker. In a sense, that is true, and every building trades worker is responsible for his own safety. No apprentice, or journeyman mechanic, should ever take any action that might cause injury to himself or to a fellow worker. Nor should he stand by and allow other workers to take such action. When it comes to safe working conditions every worker is "his brother's keeper."

Fortunately for all construction industry employees, most employers provide the necessary elements and materials for safe working conditions and insist that all safety laws, rules, and regulations be obeyed. Failure of any worker to observe common-sense working rules could be cause for dismissal.

It is always a pleasure for a safety-conscious worker to be employed on a construction project in which sensible safe working conditions are provided and safety rules rigidly enforced. Any apprentice whose first job is in a shop where safety rules are sensible and strongly enforced should be grateful for his good luck. A few months of exposure to commonsense safety rules could be instrumental in forming safety habits and attitudes that will last a lifetime.

When good attitudes toward safe working conditions can be firmly planted in the mind of the worker, that worker will be able to derive much benefit from safety meetings and safety messages. If the worker never forms good safety attitudes, and never learns to appreciate safe working conditions, safety meetings, messages, and warnings will have no effect.

Scare tactics are often used by safety engineers on construction projects, but they seem to have little effect on the heedless individual. The new apprentice might, however, keep one thought in mind—dead men and cripples bring home no paychecks, even though the insurance may console the widow.

Every occupation has its dangers, and the construction industry is no exception. With that knowledge as a guide, it should be obvious that it is just as important for an apprentice to learn to work safely as it is for him to become skilled in the use of the "tools of his trade." Probably the most important item in developing good attitudes on the subject of safe working conditions is the ability to recognize most of the dangers that may exist on every construction project. When hazards are known, they can be avoided.

The following outlines of potentially dangerous conditions that might be encountered on a construction project is not complete, but it does list many of the most obvious hazards.

Good Housekeeping

One of the most important, and often neglected, elements in any safe work program is good housekeeping. A qualified craftsman never allows his work bench or work area to become cluttered with trash, scrap material, and other debris. He never allows grease, oil, or solvent-soaked rags to accumulate in his work area, but puts such rags in a special covered container that should be provided. Oil-soaked rags should never be put in a container along with common trash such as scrap paper. The safety-conscious mechanic or apprentice will refuse to work in an area where there is substantial danger of fire, explosion, falling objects, or similar hazards. In fact, every worker should refuse to enter a construction area where such hazards are known to exist.

Ladders

Ladders are a common tool on construction jobs and a very prolific source of accidents. A safety-wise worker never uses a wooden ladder that has been painted. Paint can often cover splits and cracks in dry wood. A safety-wise worker refuses to use a ladder that has broken treads (steps), loose braces, or one that shows other signs of undue wear or weakness. When using an extension ladder the worker should make very sure that both hooks are firmly latched. The top end of a ladder should be tied to the structure to prevent slipping. In some cases it might be wise to tie the bottom end of the ladder to the structure as well. The legs of a ladder should always be set on a firm foundation, with both legs even.

Rigging and Rigging Equipment

In the building trades mechanics are often required to move heavy items of equipment and they should have some knowledge of rigging in general, wire line slings, rope slings, snatch blocks, chain falls, rope falls, hydraulic jacks, track jacks, cribbing, and so on. Extensive knowledge of rigging is not needed, as such work will usually be done by special crews, but some know-how is a must.

In rigging, a mechanic should never use a rope sling that has dried out, a wire sling that has been twisted or kinked, or any item of equipment that is in need of repair. A wise rigger will never hang a snatch block on a structure that might be pulled out of line by the strain, never allow a rope or wire line to lead over the edge of a beam, or other sharp object, never stand in the bight of a line, and never stand under a load that is being hoisted. When working with a truck crane, derrick, A-frame truck, or other types of hoisting equipment, it will be necessary to signal the operator. Standard signals have been established for every operation, and the apprentice should master their use at the earliest possible moment.

Power Tools

Apprentices and mechanics of the building trades will be required to use many types of power tools and power-driven equipment. When used with due regard for safety measures, such tools offer no hazards. Improperly used power tools, however, can be the cause of many accidents. A safety-wise worker never uses a power tool that does not have all necessary guards and shields for his protection. He never uses a grinder, sander, or other tool presenting danger from flying objects without first putting on goggles, a face shield, or both.

The safety-wise worker exercises extreme care in the use of electric- or air-powered drill motors. Even a small drill motor, if the drill bit should hang in the hole, can throw a man off a ladder or scaffold. No safety-wise worker operates an electric power tool while standing in water or on a wet floor. Never use any power tool that is not in working order.

Electrical Cords for Lights and Power Tools

Never use an extension cord that is worn or frayed. Never overload a power circuit and never throw a switch that has a MAN-ON or DANGER tag attached. Never try to do electrical repair work. Never work in an area that is not adequately lighted; in fact, refuse to work in such an area. If fuses must be changed, electrical connections made, or if more lights are needed, see to it that such work is done by a qualified electrician.

These automatic controls allow one man to operate the machinery in a 14-story building. The push buttons control temperature, mechanical equipment, and security and fire alarms. The panel alerts the operator to any malfunction, but adjustments must be made by a skilled mechanic.

Stairways, Walkways, and Catwalks

Stairways, walkways, and catwalks have but one purpose—to provide easy and unobstructed passage from one area to another, or from one elevation to another. They should never be used as a storage area for tools, material, scrap, or junk. A safety-wise worker never puts welding bottles in such passageways, and he never pulls welding leads, burner hoses, extension cords, air hoses, and the like across such passageways. In fact, there is never an excuse for placing any type of obstruction in such areas. The safety-wise worker always uses handrails that have been provided for his protection.

Manholes, Access Holes, and Excavations

The law requires a contractor to place a guard rail or fence around every hole through a floor or deck; every open pit or excavation; and any other area where a hazardous condition is known to exist. If a night operation is in progress, or if the public must pass through the area, adequate lighting must be provided.

Signs, Signals and Warning Devices

Safety engineers and employers spend a lot of time, effort, and money to develop and place foolproof signs and warning notices for the protection of workers, but if the warnings go unheeded they have little value. The safety-wise worker never ignores any safety sign, safety signal, or other warning device, and for obvious reasons: If a worker is killed or injured as a result of such oversight, he may forfeit his right, or the right of his survivors, to recover compensation under existing laws. Under no circumstances should a worker pass, or remove, a barricade to isolate an area where a hazard is known, or thought, to exist.

Handlines

On every construction project mechanics will often find it

necessary to move tools, equipment, and materials to a higher or lower level. Large items are usually moved by hoist or derrick, but small items are usually moved by hand. For that reason, a handline is an important tool on every construction job. The safety-wise worker never tries to climb a ladder with tools or material in his hands. He always uses a handline. If a number of items must be moved, a special hoisting container, or "skip," should be used. When bundles of pipe, lumber, or such are to be hoisted, and danger of slippage is present, special attention should be given to rigging.

Small Tools

Chisels, punches, star drills, shield drivers, and other tools that are driven by impact of a hammer will become split and dubbed over on the impact end. Flying fragments of metal from such tools can cause serious injury. A safety-wise worker never uses such a tool. If the tool cannot be replaced, the damaged portion should be removed by grinding, filing, or other approved method. Tools with wooden handles are potentially dangerous if the wood dries out and allows the tool to become loose on the handle. Every mechanic should make sure that the tool head is firmly fixed to the handle before using.

Safety Equipment

Employers in the construction industry are required by law to provide workers with safety equipment that will protect him against every known, or suspected, hazard. If a worker fails to use such equipment, he may forfeit his right, or the right of his survivors, to recover payment under existing compensation laws.

Goggles, face shields, and other protective devices should be worn whenever there may be the slightest danger of injury from flying objects, blowing dust, sparks, or molten material. If required, hard hats, rubber gloves, rubber aprons, and other safety equipment should be worn. In addition, every safety-wise worker should understand the dangers involved in handling acids, caustics, and toxic materials. He should also be aware of the fact that many common cleaning compounds can be harmful when used in a careless or improper manner. Improper uses include mixing stronger-than-recommended solutions, overheating, application of certain compounds on hot surfaces, inadequate ventilation, and so on.

Fires and Fire Prevention

No-smoking signs are always put up for the protection of life and property. Such signs should always be obeyed. Fire safety rules are also designed for the protection of life and property, and a safety-wise worker always follows the rules. If welding or burning must be done in an area where there is danger of fire or explosion, a fire clearance, in writing, should be obtained from the proper authority.

If a mechanic is required to burn through the shell plates of a tank, metal wall, or metal floor, he should always check to see what is on the other side. The worker should never allow grease- or oil-soaked rags to accumulate around his bench or work area. Such material should be put in a properly closed container. Oily or solvent-soaked rags should never be put in with ordinary scrap paper or trash, and a worker should never allow welding slag, sparks, or molten particles to fall into such combustible material.

Plant Operators and Building Engineers

If a building trades mechanic is working in a plant that is in operation, or a building that has tenants, he must give due notice and cooperate with the plant engineer before closing a valve or throwing a switch that would interrupt a vital service. In every instance the mechanic should make sure that he is dealing with a responsible person. That person might be the janitor, building superintendent, shift foreman, or operating engineer for the area. To act without due caution in such matters, or to proceed without authorization from someone who has the knowledge and the authority to act, could lead to costly shutdowns and severe accidents.

Safety in General

Many elements are involved in the development of a safety-wise worker, but the primary rule for every potentially hazardous situation should be: NEVER TAKE A CHANCE. Two very good reasons for never taking chances are 1. Workers, or innocent bystanders, could be injured or killed. 2. If a worker knowingly disregards safety rules and regulations, and is involved in an accident or killed, he may forfeit his right or the right of his survivors, to receive compensation for the injury or death.

If a worker on a construction project is ever in a dangerous position and he has the slightest doubt as to the course of action to be taken, he should always seek advice from his supervisor, the safety engineer, or some other responsible individual. Rarely is an emergency so critical that hasty action is justified. A careful survey of conditions is always advisable.

Questions and Answers

Q. Should a worker ever take any action that might place him or his fellow workers in danger?

A. No. Taking chances on the job is not smart. No man has a right to endanger either himself or innocent bystanders.

Q. Why is it so important for the worker to obey safety rules and regulations?

A. Accidents could cause serious injury, great suffering, or death. Dead men and cripples bring home no paychecks.

Q. Should good safety practices and procedures be a part of the training for building trades craftsmen?

A. Yes. The fact that a worker is safety-conscious and willing to abide by commonsense safety rules, is the sure indication of a skilled and mature mechanic.

Q. What are some of the important elements of good safety practices?
A. Good housekeeping is among the most important. A safety-wise mechanic never allows his work area or bench to become cluttered with trash or scrap material.

Q. Are ladders dangerous to use?
A. The answer is no, though ladders do figure in many construction job accidents. In most instances the fault lies with the way the ladder was used.

Q. Is rigging an especially hazardous part of construction work?
A. No, not if ordinary precautions are taken.

Q. What are the chief dangers to be expected in the use of power tools?
A. The chief dangers come from using a power tool that is in poor repair or that does not have safety guards in place, and failure to use protective safety equipment as indicated by job conditions.

Q. Are there special dangers in the use of electric power for power tools, lighting, construction equipment, and the like?
A. Not if commonsense rules are observed. The safety-wise worker should never use a power cord that is frayed or worn; never use a drop cord with a light bulb that does not have a protective guard, and never overload a power circuit. In addition, a worker should never close a switch that has a MAN-ON or DANGER tag attached. Electrical repairs and fuse changes should be made by a qualified electrician.

Q. Is it especially dangerous to work on a scaffold high above ground level?
A. Not if the scaffold has been properly constructed, is on a firm foundation, and ordinary precautions are taken.

Q. What care should be taken in the use of walkways, stairways, and catwalks?
A. Such passageways should be kept clear of all obstructions, scrap material, welding leads, hoses, and such.

Q. Why should warning signs, no-smoking signs, and danger notices be obeyed by every construction worker?
A. Failure to heed such signs could lead to serious accidents and injury to the individual worker, and to innocent fellow workers.

Q. Are ordinary hand tools dangerous to use?
A. Yes, such tools can be dangerous to use, if not kept in good repair, or if used in a careless manner.

Q. Must an employer supply safety equipment to protect his employees from hazardous conditions?
A. Yes, the laws of most states require it, but the worker is also required to wear such equipment.

Q. What items of safety equipment are normally supplied by the employer?
A. Requirements vary with the state, but most employers supply such items as protective goggles, face shields, hard hats, rubber gloves, rubber aprons, asbestos clothing, and welding helmets.

Q. How can a construction worker aid in fire protection?
A. The safety-wise worker never smokes in a restricted area,

never does welding or burning where a fire hazard is known to exist, and uses care in the use of all combustible materials.

Q. What is the single safety rule that should be observed by building and construction industry workers at all times?

A. That rule is simple: Never take unnecessary chances.

CHAPTER VIII

Special Financial Plans
For Construction Workers

The earning pattern for craftsmen in the construction industry differs from those of men in many other occupations with equal earning potential. That means building trades workers must take an intelligent approach to financial planning if they hope to get the most out of their vocation. During the years of his apprenticeship the building trades apprentice is paid a good wage and when he graduates to journeyman he is paid at the same rate as men who have had years of experience in the field. At first glance, it might seem that a man is starting his career at the top of his earning potential.

In reality, however, it does not work out that way. A journeyman mechanic, just out of his apprenticeship, does not immediately step into equality with more experienced mechanics. The newly graduated apprentice must prove to his employer that he is willing, and able, to assume responsibility. Under normal conditions, it usually takes a few years of "working with the tools" for a man to acquire the experience and the maturity to assume a position in which he must supervise the work of other mechanics.

It may not be apparent to the uninitiated, but it takes a certain degree of executive ability to keep even a small construction job running smoothly. Men, materials, and equipment must be scheduled to the jobsite in a manner that will ensure an even flow of work, and installation schedules must be coordinated with other contractors. Materials must be ordered, time sheets made up, and progress records kept. In fact, any building trades mechanic who elects to take jobs as a supervisor (run work) will find his job a constant challenge, seeing to it that all the elements of a job "come out even."

The gradual development of the ability to "run work" for an employer, by a journeyman who has mastered the fundamentals of his trade, is the quality that will make him a valued employee, put many extra dollars in his pay envelope, and keep him on the payroll when work is slack. In fact, pronounced ability to accept and deal with such responsibility could add from 25 to 50 percent to the lifetime earning potential of such an individual. Such ability also makes it possible for the craftsman to move from journeyman to the ownership of his own contracting business.

Not all men, however, have the desire to become supervisors, and many fine mechanics are quite content to spend their lives "working with the tools of their trade," much as a bookkeeper or shipping clerk would be content to continue working at a job he has learned to do well.

Further, there is a certain type of mechanic who has been dubbed "prima donna." Such a mechanic strives for perfection in every job and is inflexible in the standards of craftsmanship he has set for himself. As a rule the "prima donna" type of mechanic does not make a good supervisor, and the claim has been made that such men are hard to get along with, but one thing is certain: A really fine craftsman will have the respect of fellow workers and employers, no matter what his personality shortcomings may be.

Many journeymen, after a few years of working in the industry, will settle into one of the special skill jobs for which they have aptitude, and in which they can feel comfortable. When such a niche is found, even though it does cut down opportunities for advancement to some degree, such specialists may be content to remain on that level until they leave the trade. That is one of the greatest advantages offered to men who have mastered one of the building trades—the work is so varied and

The heating and air-conditioning equipment for a large commercial building graphically illustrates the craftsmanship of skilled sheet metal workers, in the duct systems, plenum chambers, and the like.

the field is so broad that there is a place for men on every level of ambition and skill.

Seasonal and Cyclical Factors

Two elements must enter into the financial planning of every man who works in the building trades—the seasonal and cyclical nature of the industry. Those two factors have been played up as constituting a serious drawback, but the truth is that they are not all to the bad.

It is known that the industry has always been subject to boom-and-bust periods, but in recent years the amount of service, maintenance, and repair work done by building trades mechanics has increased to such a point that a much more predictable level of employment can be achieved. Of course, some periods of slack construction activity will always occur, and severe weather conditions can bring some types of building work to a halt, but certain factors offer compensation.

At times the seasonal and cyclical nature of the industry can work to the workers' advantage. That occurs when a customer has decided to get a new plant ready for production ahead of contract completion date; when an office building must be made ready for occupancy before the scheduled completion date; when construction is behind schedule, and the contractor has a penalty clause in his contract; and when construction is hurried to avoid working in severe weather.

It does not take many weeks of premium pay for overtime to make up for time lost because of slack construction activity, but no building trades worker should base his financial planning on the hope of overtime pay. Overtime and premium pay should be a "kicker" to the many advantages offered to workers in the industry because it helps to level out the yearly earning pattern.

It is a sad fact that many building trades workers never seem to understand fully the seasonal and cyclical nature of construction. When the boom is on they joyfully spend every dime they make; when the slack periods come, as they always do, financial problems multiply, and cuts must be made.

For obvious reasons, men who work in a seasonal and cyclical business should not estimate income on a month-to-month basis. Their rates for spending should be based on annual income, and the estimates for annual income should be spread over a minimum of three years. As a rule, by the time a man has completed a five-year apprenticeship, he should be able to gauge the earning patterns for construction workers in his locality.

Fringe Benefits

One relationship that exists between a building trades worker, his employer, and his local union is strictly business, and should always be treated in a businesslike manner. That relationship has to do with the fringe benefits a construction worker receives under the provisions of the contract between the local union and the employers. Those fringe benefits are an extension of the worker's income, but they often have an importance far greater than might be indicated by the amounts of money involved. Some of the benefits come to the worker as a result of his union contract with the employers. Others come to him because of state or federal laws, but all are important.

Health and Welfare Insurance

Every member of a building trades union should understand the provisions of the health insurance program provided by his local union and paid for by his employer or employers. He should know how many hours must be worked in a given period to be covered by the insurance, and he should understand the benefits available, the amount deductible for each illness, and which health problems are not covered by his policy.

Health and welfare plans in local unions have been the source of much dissension in the past—because the average union member never takes the time to read the fine print and become fully informed of his rights. The master policy may not always be available to the average member, but the trustees of the plan send out information bulletins telling of all changes in coverage, effective date of changes, and so on. Every member has a duty to himself, and to his family, to be informed on the subject. (The board of trustees is made up of an equal number of members from the local union and the employers. In most instances the same board of trustees will administer all fringe benefit trust funds of the local union.)

Vacation Pay

Most local unions now have some provision for paid vacations. The amount received is usually based on the number of hours worked by the individual member during the past calendar or fiscal year, with a lag period of from three to six months to allow for collecting from contractors and bookkeeping. The number of hours of vacation credited each week is noted on the paycheck stub or voucher. Mistakes do happen, and it is of vital importance for each worker to save his paycheck stubs. The best source of information on the subject of vacation pay is the office of the local union.

Pensions

Most local unions have some form of pension plan for members, but qualification for such plans is not always automatic, and the individual member has a responsibility to look after his own rights. There is never an intent to deprive members of benefits, but certain provisions must be met. The pension and retirement plans of building trades local unions are often quite complex, and every member should be on guard against taking any action that could cause him to lose benefits.

Unlike Social Security, many local union pension plans do not follow members who transfer to another local, or who move to an area outside the jurisdiction of the plan. If that happens, and the pension plan is not transferable, years of pension credit and retirements could be lost. Under some pension plans a member does "nail down" certain minimum benefits after a long period of continuous coverage, but vested rights should never be taken for granted.

A great deal of variation exists between the pension plans of building trades local unions, and nothing should be taken for granted. Every member who is covered by such a plan should inform himself of the provisions of his pension plan lest he take some hasty action that might cause his benefits to be lost by default. If a union member is considering any action that might affect his pension benefits, vested rights, or such, he would be well advised to consult a lawyer before making a decision.

Group Insurance

Local unions may have several forms of group life insurance on the lives of members and their dependents. Such insurance might include a death benefit paid by the national union; a death benefit fund of the local union paid by assessment on members for each death; group life insurance paid for by members; life insurance that is a part of the health insurance program of the local union, or others.

Such group insurance, no matter what the type, is always a bargain for union members and should be kept paid up. Information about group insurance can be obtained at the office of the local union. Every union member should have an up-to-date beneficiary card on file at the local office. Failure to update beneficiaries after any change of status could mean loss of benefits to survivors. In fact, many cases are on record in which group insurance has been paid to the wrong person because a member failed to change his beneficiary after a divorce, remarriage, death of a beneficiary, or similar status change.

State and National Insurance Laws

Certain insurance benefits are available under state and federal laws, and every union member should have some knowledge of his rights under those laws. He need not have extensive information, but he should be on notice that the laws do exist, where to apply for benefits, and how to file a claim. If a worker, or the dependent of an injured or deceased worker should have occasion to file a claim under the provisions of those laws, it might be wise to consult a lawyer.

Workmen's Compensation

Nearly every state now has some form of Workmen's Compensation law to cover the worker who is injured, killed, or becomes ill as a direct result of his job. The law is usually administered by a state commission, which may have offices in many cities and towns. If a worker is injured on the job, and does not receive good medical attention, or believes his rights have been denied, he should get in touch with the agents of the State Accident Commission. Benefits available to workers under Workmen's Compensation laws include all hospital and medical bills for on-the-job, or job-related, injuries; cash payments based on a percentage of wages; death benefits; and so forth.

Social Security

Nearly every worker knows of the benefits available under the provisions of federal Social Security, but many workers may not understand all of the provisions of the law. Social Security benefits include retirement benefits; disability benefits; death benefits; survivors' benefits, which may include a surviving spouse, minor children, guardians of minor children, parents, and the like.

One point should be made clear to every worker: Benefits cannot be paid if a claim is not filed, and the best place to get information on the subject is at the local office of the Social Security Administration.

Unemployment Compensation

Nearly every state now has some form of insurance to tide the worker over periods of unemployment. The amount paid per week, number of weeks paid, and eligibility for payment varies from state to state. The best place to obtain information on the subject is the Unemployment Insurance Commission (sometimes called the Employment Security Department).

Eligibility for benefits and amount of benefits are based on payroll records. The funds are paid by the employer to the commission, and the worker has no control over the records, but if an employer fails to remit, or an error has been made in the account, the weekly payroll statements received by the employee will be the single most important piece of evidence the worker will have to force a quick accounting. Payroll statements, often referred to as check stubs, are of vital importance to every building and construction industry worker.

Disability Insurance

Many states have a disability law that makes it possible for a worker who is off the job because of a non-work-related accident or illness to receive a percentage of his wages each week in the form of a check from the Disability Insurance Commission. Eligibility and amount of benefits paid vary, and the office of the commission is the best place to get information. As is the case with unemployment insurance, the employer pays money into the disability fund. The worker has no control over those records, but if the employer fails to pay into the fund, or if an error has been made, payroll statements (check stubs) offer the best proof of benefits earned, dates earned, amount earned, and such. In fact, payroll statements that come with each paycheck contain proof of so much important information that it is of vital importance for every employee to keep such records for a minimum of three years.

Questions and Answers

Q. Why is it important for workers in the building and construction industry to give special attention to financial matters?

A. Construction is a seasonal and cyclical business. The worker should base his budgeting of income and expenditures on annual earnings, rather than on weekly or monthly income.

Q. When an apprentice graduates to journeyman, is his earning capacity equal to that of more experienced mechanics?
A. No. His basic wage rate may be the same, but the seasoned worker will probably have steadier employment; may receive premium pay for special duties; or may receive the higher wage rates paid to foremen, general foremen, or other supervisors.

Q. What is meant when it is said that an apprentice "takes the tools"?
A. When an apprentice graduates to journeyman it is said that he has "taken the tools of his trade." That means he will no longer be working under the supervision of a journeyman and must now assume greater responsibility.

Q. What is meant by the term, "working with the tools"?
A. When a building trades mechanic begins to use the tools of his trade, he is said to be "working with the tools." If a journeyman takes a job as instructor, inspector, estimator, or supervisor it is said that he has "left the tools." If he gives up his foremanship or similar job, it is said that he "goes back to the tools." It is the right and the privilege of every building trades craftsman to work with the tools of his trade for as long as he works in the industry.

Q. How can the seasonal and cyclical factors of the construction industry work to the advantage of building trades workers?
A. In many ways. If a new plant can be rushed into production a few weeks ahead of schedule, or if an office or hotel building can be made ready for occupancy before the regular opening date, contractors will often work construction crews

overtime at premium wage rates. The same thing can happen when a construction project is behind schedule and a penalty clause is part of the contract. Severe weather conditions can also be a factor.

Q. Are the fringe benefits that are paid to building trades workers under the terms of the contract between the local building union and the employers an important part of overall pay?
A. Fringe benefits are a vital part of the pay rates to those workers.

Q. Would the same amount of money in cash, or added to the worker's paycheck, have an equivalent value?
A. The answer is a very definite NO, but many workers do not fully understand that fact. Group insurance is always cheaper than equivalent insurance bought by an individual. In addition, there is always the possibility that the individual will fail to pay a premium on time. If that should happen and a worker, or one of his dependents, should suffer a serious injury or illness, financial disaster could follow.

Q. Is the same true of union pension plans?
A. True, only more so. Pension plans are a form of forced savings that take nothing away from the worker's paycheck. If a younger worker should doubt the value of pension plans, he might ask the retired worker who is drawing retirement benefits. (It might be even more revealing to ask the opinion of the retired worker who did not qualify for retirement benefits.)

Q. How can a building trades worker get the most out of the health and welfare plan negotiated for him by his local union?
A. By knowing how the plan works, and by keeping up with changes that may be made from year to year.

Q. Are health and welfare plans of local unions often the cause of dissension among union members?

A. Yes, health and welfare plans can cause trouble, but it is seldom the fault of the plan. Many union members pay no attention to the provisions of union insurance plans until they have need of them. When that occurs, such members often expect the insurance plan to cover expenses not included in the health and welfare insurance contract.

Q. Are there state and federal labor and insurance laws of which every building trades workers should have some knowledge?

A. Yes, many such laws are vitally important to every construction worker.

Q. Does that mean every worker should get a copy of the laws and study them?

A. No, that would not be necessary for most workers. The important factor is for the worker to know that such laws are available for his protection, and to know where to go to get information and assistance.

Q. How do Workmen's Compensation laws affect the worker?

A. Under the laws of most states, employers are required to carry insurance that will cover hospital and medical costs, plus a percentage of wages, for every on-the-job injury or illness caused by job-related activities. Death benefits for survivors are usually among the benefits offered under such coverage.

Q. Social Security benefits have been well publicized, and most workers are aware of retirement payments, but what other benefits come to the worker under Social Security laws?

A. Under certain conditions a worker might be eligible to draw disability retirement benefits; death payment benefits; or benefits for surviving spouse, minor children, guardians of minor children, aged parents, and the like.

Q. How can a union member keep his health and welfare insurance coverage during periods of unemployment or protracted illness?

A. Many local union health and welfare plans have a provision for the worker to continue his benefit eligibility during such periods by paying the premiums in advance. The action must, however, be initiated by the worker. It is seldom automatic.

Q. How can a worker keep a record of his vacation and holiday benefits?

A. Vacation benefits are often based on hours worked or paid. The number of hours credited to vacation benefits will be equal to the number of hours worked or paid. (There are exceptions.) Such information is usually included on payroll statements that come with each paycheck.

Q. Why should every worker have some knowledge of the pension plan available through his local union?

A. It is important to have such knowledge in order to be able to avoid actions that might cause loss of retirement benefits. Those might include such actions as quitting the union, transfer to another local union, or moving to another state. Pension plans are often quite complex, and hasty actions can cause the loss of valuable benefits. It might be wise to consult a lawyer or other authority before making a serious move. Such consultation should be before the action is taken —not after.

Q. Is there one single habit a worker can form that may save him time, effort, and loss of fringe benefits?

A. Yes. The habit of saving payroll statements that ccme with each paycheck. Those statements contain information not included on W-2 forms and other tax statements.

CHAPTER IX

Local Unions

The building and construction trades unions have more than 3,000,000 members comprising several national unions with very large memberships and a number of smaller national organizations, plus several thousand local unions. It would not be possible to give constitutional and structural variations of all those national and local unions, but the information presented here is of a very general nature and will apply to most local union operations.

Union Tradition

The dictionary defines tradition as "the handing down of information . . . by word of mouth or by example . . . without written instruction." In that sense it can truly be said that the building and construction trades unions have a fine and well-earned tradition.

The building trades unions of the United States and Canada have a great heritage that has been passed down from the early days of trade unionism. The traditions of those unions have grown out of their maintenance of high standards of craftsmanship, service to the community, and devotion to a cause. The purposes of trade unions have always been to develop skilled craftsmen, to meet the challenge of change, and to serve the nation and the community.

Over the past decades science has brought many changes and technological developments, and with those changes has come the need for craftsmen of the building trades to develop new, and higher, degrees of skill. It is no longer possible for a young man to serve out his apprenticeship and graduate to journeyman with the serene expectation that he is all set in a lifetime vocation. In this technical age every building trades craftsman must constantly upgrade his skills if he hopes to remain competitive. The constructive and far-sighted actions of pioneer union leaders have made it possible for trade union members of today to live and work with dignity and self-respect, and to share in the wealth they have helped to produce. That is a fine heritage, but if the craftsmen of this generation do not continue the constructive effort, past gains may be lost by default.

Present-day trade union men are custodians of the good that has been given to them by past generations, in the same sense that every citizen benefits from constructive efforts made by statesmen of the past. Good unionism has many detractors, just as there are many detractors of good citizenship, but those evil forces should not be allowed to take away the high principles that men enjoy under a democratic form of government.

The Pledge in Union Membership

When a man takes on the obligation of membership in a building trades union he will be required to take a pledge. He must promise to abide by the constitution and by-laws of his local union, including all constitutional provisions in effect at the time and those that may be enacted at some future date.

A local union of the building trades is operated under democratic principles, and that can work only when each and every union member understands that the real good is the good of the majority. Any union member who tries to gain personal advantage at the expense of fellow union members is breaking his pledge.

For those reasons it is very important for every candidate for membership in a building trades local union to examine the constitution, by-laws, and working rules of the union he expects to join to determine if any part of the method of operation might conflict with his personal code of ethics and morality. If such

The engineering department of a large contractor, where thousands of blueprints and working drawings are made, which, along with the specifications, spell out every detail of construction for a large project.

conflict does exist, and the individual learns that he has deep-seated feelings of conflict, it might be wise for that man to seek a vocation in which union membership is not a requirement.

The pledge the candidate will be asked to take is quite a simple one. It does not threaten the man with drastic punishment if he fails to live up to his obligation, but it does put him on his honor to abide by the ideals, ethical standards, and standards of craftsmanship of his union.

The candidate must promise to attend union meetings, and he must never divulge official union business to unauthorized persons. He further promises to cultivate a feeling of respect and friendship for his brother union members, and to come to the assistance of any brother who might be in need. The candidate must also swear that he is not now, and has never been, a member of any subversive organization. The candidate takes the pledge voluntarily and should have no mental reservations.

The union member is bound by his oath, or pledge, to his union until death or honorable withdrawal. The terms of withdrawal from membership in a building trades union should be understood by every member, but often are not. A provision in every local union constitution allows a member to withdraw from membership. In most instances withdrawal can be temporary or permanent. Of course, if a union member simply stops paying dues and assessments, he will be dropped from the rolls of the organization after a time, although that type of withdrawal could mean a loss of built-up benefits. Formal withdrawal makes it possible to regain membership without penalty, and certain benefits that have accrued, such as pension rights and insurance rights, may be protected.

The pledge is not intended to cause a union member to forsake any duty he may have to his family, country, or personal ethics. When the candidate takes the pledge, and is initiated into membership in a local union, he receives all of the rights and all the respect due under union membership. By the same token, he is expected to assume all the responsibilities involved in union membership.

Good Trade Unionism and Good Citizenship

Good trade unionism and good citizenship go hand in hand, with never a conflict between the two. Members of building trades unions probably receive more political education than many other economic groups. Both local and national unions make an effort to keep their members informed on the subject of business conditions, pending legislation that might affect the construction industry, voting records of office seekers and incumbents, and the political scene in general.

In this fast-moving age, when state and national laws affect the lives of every citizen, it is important for everyone to be informed. Since much of the information supplied to members by local and national unions is rather general and concerned with larger issues, it may be less biased and self-seeking than information released for local consumption by business interests and candidates for political office.

Certain factions within the United States would foster the belief that certain labor leaders can deliver the vote of their memberships to certain candidates and specific issues. That could never be true of the men who work in the building and construction industry. Most of the men are skilled craftsmen, and the skilled craftsman is a very independent individual. He wears no man's collar, and no man could deliver his vote.

It has been charged that labor leaders are selfish in their efforts to gain recognition, better wages, and better working conditions for union members. If that charge is true, then they share the guilt with the A.M.A., P. T.A., Farm Bureau, Federation of Teachers, League of Ministers, and many similar organizations. There is nothing wrong with an organization of individuals who work to better the lot of the group—except, of course, if such gains are made at the expense of others.

A local union of the building trades is an example of democracy in action. Every local union has local autonomy and is governed by its members. It has its own constitution, by-laws, and working rules and elects its own officers. Every local union member in good standing has the right, and the duty, to attend meetings and run for office. The constitution of the local union is under constant debate, and all rules are subject to change by the will of the majority. Every election of officers, and every vote on important issues, is decided by a secret ballot.

Conduct of Union Members

Trade unionism is a way of life, and any man who commits himself to this philosophy should understand his responsibility to his union and to his union brothers. An apprentice who is just starting to master a trade may feel that he is far removed from responsibility for operation of his local union, but he must be made to understand that in the not too distant future he will be in the driver's seat. For that reason, the time to start preparation for responsible action in that area is the first day on the job as an apprentice.

The only realistic way to learn how a local union operates is to observe that segment of trade unionism in action. That can be done by attending regular union meetings and by taking part in union activities. Probably the most important step toward preparation for responsibility should come when the candidate decides to accept trade unionism as a way of life. Union members should always be grateful for the fact that they are free to join, or not to join, a labor organization—a privilege denied to workers in many parts of the world.

Men become members of a labor organization for many reasons, and they come from all walks of life, but most men join because they welcome the advantages that union membership will bring. A few men, however, seek membership in a labor union for purely selfish reasons, and there have been cases in which such self-seeking individuals have gained high office. Such

A tanker begins to shape up, six months after keel-laying, although bow and stern sections are not yet in place. Work of this sort involves all the building trades, with the boilermakers very active at this stage of construction.

office-seekers use a gift of gab and clever political tactics to gain votes from an apathetic membership. When elected to responsible office, such men often gather about them men of their own ilk and take over the entire operation. When that happens great harm can come to the local union and to organized labor in general. Fortunately, greed may soon destroy them, but not before much damage to union prestige has been done.

It has been charged that minority groups, or cliques, control the operation of many local unions of the building trades, but if only 20 or 30 percent of the members of a local union attend meetings, a minority is forced to assume responsibility for its operation. That is not a good way to run a union, but members should be grateful to the dedicated minority who faithfully attend meetings, serve on committees, and hold office. Those trade union men give their time and their best effort, without hope or expectation of pay, and often with little recognition. If every union member would assume his share of the responsibility, there would soon be an end to minority rule in union operation.

Rights of Union Members

Every member of a local union should have a working knowledge of the constitution, by-laws, and working agreements of his union. Most union members accept the idea of the good of the majority and never try to use the union for their own selfish ends. If a union member accepts that idea, he will never be in trouble with his union, but if he does break the rules he may be in trouble. Ignorance of the rules is never an excuse.

If a local union member does have charges filed against him, he should know how to conduct himself during the investigation and hearing. In most instances a union will try to avoid filing formal charges against a member. Warnings and reprimands may be given, and informal hearings may be held, but if nothing can be done to induce the offending member to mend his ways, then formal charges must be filed.

Certain formalities must be observed in filing charges and

should always be taken seriously. The member who makes the charge should be a member in good standing. The charges must be in writing, and there should be one or more witnesses, if possible. The exact location where the violation of rules took place, usually a jobsite, should be given, plus the exact time of day, date, and other pertinent information. The nature of the violation should be stated, with notations of the section of the union constitution that applies.

When the charges are presented to the union membership, usually at the next regular meeting, they must be read in full. In most instances, after the charges have been read, explained, and discussed, a motion will be made, and the membership will vote for the charges to take the "usual course." That means the matter will go to the Executive Board for investigation.

If the investigation shows the charges to be sound, a date for a hearing will be set. A copy of the charges, stamped with the official seal of the local union, must be delivered to the member charged. If the offender cannot be found, a copy of the charges will be mailed to his latest address of record.

The offender is expected to appear at the hearing and to present a defense. He will be allowed to present any mitigating circumstances, and he may produce witnesses to support his claims. All evidence will be considered, and if the man is found guilty, the Executive Board will recommend punishment. If he is found not guilty, the charges will be dismissed, and the membership will be informed of the action at the next regular meeting. Punishment must be in compliance with local and national union constitution and by-laws.

The recommendations for punishment made by the Executive Board will be read to the membership, and, if the majority approve, findings will be entered into the record, but subject to appeal. Provisions are made in the constitutions of all local and national unions for appeal from all punishment, except for such things as minor fines. If the punishment should be severe, such as expulsion or a large fine, it would be wise for the accused to

The container ship Hawaiian Citizen *being loaded at a Honolulu dock. Such containers are a new development in shipping and have added thousands of jobs to the building trades.*

seek expert counsel, such as a lawyer or a union brother who is versed in hearing procedures, union laws, and appeals. The offender also has the right to appeal to a civil court, but he should first exhaust every avenue of appeal open to him under local and national constitutions and by-laws.

Apprentice Rights

Apprentice members have been known to complain because they have no voice or vote in union affairs, but that is not justified. During his apprenticeship the apprentice is not considered to be under direct control of the local union. He is subject to the authority of the Joint Apprenticeship Committee, and that committee will be responsible for disciplinary action, or hear any appeal.

The apprentice must earn the right to a voice and vote in the same manner that he learns the fundamentals of his trade and good craftsmanship—under the guidance and instruction of senior members. The gradual absorption of the principles of good trade unionism is a normal and very important part of every apprentice-training program, but this is a hard point to make. Apprentices must be made to understand that in the not too distant future they will have the responsibility of running the local union.

Questions and Answers

Q. What is meant by trade union tradition?

A. Tradition of good trade unionism means the passing on of high ideals, high standards of craftsmanship, and the need for personal integrity in all work and union activities.

Q. Do present-day union members have an important part to play in the preservation of union tradition?

A. They have more than a part to play—they must preserve present tradition and lay the foundation for the tradition of the future.

Q. Will present-day union members be given credit for preserving union tradition?

A. Union members do not look for credit for such service. Their satisfaction comes from knowing that they have met their responsibility.

Q. Do present-day union members have it as tough as men did in the early days of the movement?

A. They do not have it tough in the sense that they may face jail or violent attack to gain their ends. The job of modern-day trade union members is a custodial one. There will never be a time when labor unions will be able to relax their vigilant efforts to promote the welfare of their members. Detractors of trade unionism are always busy, and they can have great appeal to the naive or uninformed.

Q. How can the individual union member help to uphold the traditions and ideals of his union?

A. By being always on guard against the enemies of his union. In most instances those enemies are not the employers, or the law, but those who seek to gain some selfish benefit. Apathy on the part of union members often gives such selfish interests the only weapon they need.

Q. Why is a candidate required to take a pledge when he joins a union?

A. He takes the pledge to prove that he is aware of, and willing to accept, the responsibility that goes with membership in a labor union.

Q. What penalty is leveled against a member who breaks his pledge?

A. He will be known as a man who is unworthy of trust. In addition, he might be subject to suspension, expulsion, or fine.

Q. Should a candidate for union membership take the pledge lightly?

A. Never. The pledge should be taken only after a careful examination of all it involves.

Q. Does a candidate have a chance to learn the responsibility of union membership before he takes the pledge?

A. Yes, every candidate is given an opportunity to read the constitution, by-laws, and working agreements of the local union he expects to join.

Q. Will a candidate be required to state that he is not a member of any subversive organization?

A. Yes, such a clause is included in the pledge for most local unions of the building and construction trades.

Q. When a man takes the pledge required for union membership does he give up any of his rights as a citizen?

A. No.

Q. When a man takes a pledge to join a building trades union is he bound for life?

A. No. Every union constitution has a provision for honorable withdrawal. Nonpayment of dues will, in time, have the same result.

Q. Is there anything in the constitution and by-laws of a building trades union that would prevent a man from being a good citizen?

A. No. On the contrary, membership in such unions should make a man more aware of his responsibilities to his country. The right to join, or not to join, a union is the right of every citizen.

Q. Do union members take note of the voting records of those politicians who hold public office?

A. Yes, and they have this idea in common with every informed voter: They believe a candidate for office should run on his real record, not the record he tries to present at election time.

Q. Are the leaders of construction industry unions able to force their members to vote as they direct?
A. No. Skilled craftsmen are very independent individuals. It is ridiculous to believe that they would vote as directed.

Q. Are union members apt to be well informed?
A. Yes. Construction activity cuts across every segment of trade and industry.

Q. Why should members of a building trades local union have an understanding of a democratic form of government?
A. Because his union is run on democratic principles. By observing his union in action he sees the democratic process in action.

Q. Do small minority groups control the operation of most local unions?
A. That is a common charge, but there is little truth in it.

Q. If that is true, why is the charge made?
A. It is made because only a certain percentage of all union members attend union meetings and engage in union activities. Very often the so-called cliques in local unions are made up of the most dedicated union members, those who seek only to serve the cause of good trade unionism.

Q. Should the members of a building trades union cooperate with, and seek the good will of, members of other unions?
A. Certainly. All right-thinking union members have a common cause.

Q. Do members of a building trades union have a responsibility to the public?
A. Of course. Every craftsman is required to be qualified for his trade, courteous to all customers, and to try to build a better image for his vocation.

Q. Should union members patronize union shops and look for the union label on the products they buy?
A. Certainly. People who support organized labor should be given the support of labor.

Q. Should union members support every business and every political candidate who claims to be for organized labor?
A. No. He should support only those who have been proven worthy of support.

Q. Does ignorance of union rules and regulations excuse a member who breaks those rules?
A. No. Ignorance of union rules is no excuse.

Q. Will the punishment for breaking union rules be severe?
A. There are minor and major infractions. A minor infraction might call for a warning, reprimand, or small fine. A major charge might bring a large fine, suspension, or expulsion.

Q. Does a member of a building trades union have a duty to report a union brother he knows to be in serious violation of union rules?
A. Failure to act might be cause for a charge of dereliction of duty.

Q. Must formal charges against a union member be put in writing?
A. Yes, all charges must be written. An anonymous charge will not be accepted.

Q. If an offender is found guilty, does he have any right of appeal?

A. Yes, there are several avenues of appeal, and all major findings are automatically reviewed by an impartial board.

Q. Is an apprentice member subject to the same rules as a journeyman member?

A. Yes, the apprentice is expected to abide by all rules.

Q. Why is an apprentice union member denied the right to a voice and vote in union affairs?

A. The apprentice must earn the right to a voice and vote in his union by completing his apprenticeship.

National Unions

The relationship that exists between a local union of the building trades and the national union for each trade is set out in detail in the constitution and by-laws of each union. The structure and method of operation vary somewhat in detail from one local-national union to another, but the basic concepts are much the same.

In essence, the national union is the governing body, with the power to issue, or withdraw, charters for local unions. Most local unions of the building trades have a high degree of autonomy, with their own constitution, by-laws, dues structure, and the right to elect all local union officials. In every instance, however, local union structure and operating rules must conform to the constitution and by-laws of the national union.

The national unions of the building trades will issue a charter for a local union in any area in which one is needed. The national union does hold absolute control over local unions, but seldom interferes in local union affairs. About the only cause for takeover of a local union would be a local's attempt to exceed its authority, calling too many unauthorized strikes, attracting too much public notice, or having too many jurisdictional disputes with other labor organizations. When a national union does find it necessary to take action, results often surprise local union officials and members.

Union members who are well informed on local/national union relationships often complain because their local union is owned by the national union, but the local union does not have the same ownership rights in the national union. In actual practice, if a local union is functioning well and meeting its obligations, there is seldom cause for complaint. On the other hand, if a local union becomes too ambitious, the crackdown can be swift and sure.

Trouble sometimes develops when two or more local unions are merged into a single unit. In such instances one or more of the local unions must lose its identity, and all money and property come under the control of the surviving local. Cases have occurred in which members of a local union have voted to sell off property and divide assets among members. It always comes as a shock when the members discover that they do not hold title to such assets.

That may seem unfair, but it is probably the only method that will prevent local unions from quitting the national union when trouble develops. If quitting were allowed, the fractioning of union structure would weaken the entire labor movement. With this one exception, most national unions serve their local unions well.

Service to local unions by the national unions includes a staff of skilled general organizers who work to maintain and increase union membership and provide a means for instant communication between local and national union officials.

In addition most national unions have a staff of lawyers and lobbyists who work in Washington, D.C., and in many state capitals. Organized labor is under constant attack, and without the support of the national organization even the largest local unions would be vulnerable.

Most national unions publish a monthly journal that is sent free of charge to all local union members. The magazine publishes news items, reports of national/local union activities, employment opportunities, and such. Special departments include obituaries, special announcements, convention calls, consumer advice, training material, and many other items of special interest to union members in the United States and Canada.

One of the more important functions of the national unions

The machine shown above, patterned after similar machines used in high-way construction, was especially designed for laying concrete linings in canals. The work involves mechanics from many of the building trades. Although the drivers of the transit-mix, water and flatbed trucks (top) are members of the Teamsters union, they are not considered part of the build-ing trades.

is to provide a national working agreement that can be signed by contractors who operate on a national scale. The national contract gives protection to the contractors when they must bid jobs in isolated areas where no large pool of skilled manpower is available. With that contract the employer has a solid base under his figures for wages, fringe benefits, travel time, transportation, and the like. Without such a solid base such contractors would be at a great disadvantage.

Many local union members and officials resent the national contracts because they believe the intent is to undercut local union wages and working conditions. That idea is false: The national contracts protect both management and labor. A small local union would not have either the experience or the resources to police a large construction project. Under such conditions labor-management relationships could break down. If that should happen, a move might be made to set up an independent union to function for the duration of a single construction project.

In the past, such independent unions were common, but they never worked out very well for either management or labor, mostly because no independent union would be able to supply the large numbers of skilled craftsmen required to man a large construction project.

The general organizers who are maintained in the field by all of the national unions of the building trades serve both management and labor in many ways. They act as referees in jurisdictional disputes; serve both sides in pre-job conferences at which questions of jurisdiction and work assignments are worked out in advance. The general organizers are usually better qualified to deal with labor problems than the officials of a small local union.

Some of the problems that occur on large construction projects, especially when such projects are in newly developed industrial areas, come about because of the following conditions. When a large project is built in an isolated area where no large pool of skilled labor is available, construction workers are drawn from many parts of the country. Wage rates, fringe benefits, work assignments, and working conditions vary in every section of the country from which men are drawn, which often leads to misunderstandings, jurisdictional disputes, and other labor troubles.

Under such conditions it is often difficult to make the workers understand that they are not working under labor contracts such as are in force in their home area. The general organizers can be of assistance in such situations because they have had extensive experience in the field, have knowledge of jurisdictional matters, and know what precedents have been set in past disputes. What may be of even more importance is the fact that they can avoid setting precedents that might be used at some later date to the detriment of their local or national unions.

On any large construction project for which craftsmen are drawn from other areas, many viewpoints vie for recognition, and disputes can occur. Tempers may run high, and jobs can be delayed by walkouts and wildcat strikes. Such unauthorized acts gain little for organized labor and they place a great amount of stress on management-labor relationships. Most of the disputes could be avoided if the men on the job would turn to the national union and its staff of skilled general organizers for advice and counsel.

Most members of building trades unions believe that they have a duty to act as shop steward in every activity that might affect the welfare of their local union. In a sense that is true, especially on small jobs to which no regular shop steward is assigned, but every union member should hesitate to take any action that might be detrimental to his local or national union or to organized labor in general.

No individual union member, or group of union members, has the right to agitate for a strike or walkout that is not authorized by the proper authorities. Well-defined procedures exist for the settlement of nearly every dispute and should be used. In

Trenching machines of the type shown above, operated by one man with the assistance of an oiler (left), are an important element in many construction projects.

some instances the dispute can be settled by arbitration at the jobsite. In other instances settlement can be achieved only be means of a conference between management, local union officials, general organizers, and other officials of the national union.

The national unions for every craft stand ready to come to the assistance of their local unions whenever the need arises, but those busy labor and management representatives should never be called in to deal with trifling disputes that often have their origin in individual personality clashes. In the matter of union-management relationships, irresponsible actions can do much harm. A very large percentage of all minor labor problems that occur at the jobsite could be settled by commonsense actions of men at the scene.

Questions and Answers

Q. How is a local union of the building trades related to the national union for each craft?

A. The relationship that exists between national/local unions of the building trades is similar in nature to that of any trade or fraternal organization. The national union operates on the national level and sets overall policy. Local unions have a considerable degree of local autonomy, with power to deal with local labor problems.

Q. How can the national unions be of assistance to their local unions?

A. Probably the most important area of assistance is the representation they afford in Washington, D.C., and state capitals where most labor legislation originates.

Q. Do the national unions of the building trades work to develop a good public image for union members and organized labor in general?

A. They do some work in the public relations field on the national level, but often neglect that important field on the local level.

Q. What other types of help can the national unions offer their local unions?

A. All of the national unions have a staff of trained general organizers, lawyers, and other consultants who offer advice, assistance and counsel to local union officials on many subjects.

Q. Why do most national unions for the building trades publish a monthly magazine or journal?

A. The journals (publications) print news items, reports, and special announcements and developments of interest to union members in every section of the United States and Canada.

Q. Why do most national unions of the building trades offer a national working agreement to certain national and international construction contractors?

A. Such national working agreements (contracts) give protection to contractors who must bid jobs in isolated areas where no large pool of skilled labor is available.

Q. Do those national contracts conflict with local union working agreements?

A. No. They are not meant to conflict in any way. On the contrary, they may give a small local union better control over work assignments and jurisdiction of work.

Q. How could a national contract help a local union to control a large construction project?

A. The very large local unions of the building trades, most of which are located in established industrial areas, usually have the resources and know-how to police a large construction job, but smaller local unions must look to the resources of the national union.

Q. How can a general organizer from the staff of the national union be of assistance to a local union?

A. One important area of assistance is the pre-job conference at which labor and management get together to work out jurisdiction and job assignments. The general organizers have extensive experience in the field, know labor law, and the rules of area practice. They know what precedents have been set in the past and they know how to avoid setting precedents that might come back to haunt them in the future.

Q. Should any member of a local union take independent actions that might involve his union in a wildcat strike or walkout?

A. Never. Every union member has a duty to report wrong actions by management, fellow local union members, or members of other labor organizations to the proper authority, but he should never try to initiate direct action.

Q. Would it be a good idea for every local union of the building trades to stay on good terms with the general organizers for his national union?

A. By all means. The general organizers can help local union officials and members in many ways, but they are busy men and should never be called in to settle trifling disputes.

Q. Will the general organizers meddle in the affairs of a local union?

A. Never. A general organizer will act only when ordered to do so by the president of the national union or other authorized official.

(*Note:* The subject of national local union relationships is very complex and only the briefest outline has been presented here.

It should be noted, however, that full information on the structure and operation of local/national unions is open to all union members who care to investigate. Unfortunately, all too few bother to do so.)

CHAPTER XI

Case Histories

When using the lives of real people to illustrate the career possibilities in any field, the strong inclination is to stick to stories of men who have achieved a notable success. That is inevitable because it takes time to master the fundamentals of any job, plus a few years of experience to gain proficiency and acquire the mature attitudes that make it possible to assume substantial responsibility. In some instances, however, certain individuals reveal the potential for success at an early stage in their careers.

Bob Y. was such a man, and his story is of especial interest because his career was deeply involved in labor union activities. He became interested in the subject while still an apprentice and went on to become Business Manager of a local union for the building trades. Not every man who takes an interest in union politics will go on to become head of a local union, but every union member should expect to hold office in his local and take an interest in every aspect of union activity.

The Bob Y. Story

Bob Y. was not born with a silver spoon in his mouth, but his parents were well off and seemed determined to indulge every whim of an only child. Bob was not exactly handsome, but he had a shock of curly blond hair, blue eyes, strong, even teeth, and a slightly too pointed nose. The one thing that detracted from his good looks was a small smile that could quickly turn into a disdainful sneer when he was displeased. In appearance Bob was deceptive. Five feet seven and deep through the chest, he looked like a trim 165 pounds, but his actual weight was 185 pounds.

Bob was popular with the girls, but took no part in school sports or political activities, and he was smart enough to keep up his grades without too much strain. When he was old enough to have a driver's license his folks bought him a sports car. Bob didn't just drive the car, but always took off with a rush and with rubber burning. When he stopped for a red light it always seemed as if the car might stand on its nose, and he would "drag" with anyone when the light turned green. Appearances must have been deceptive, however, for, in spite of all the dire predictions of family and friends, he was never in a serious accident, and any tickets he got were for minor violations.

The year he graduated from high school Bob decided to learn a trade and somehow managed to become an apprentice in one of the unions for the building trades. He was a good worker and got along pretty well with fellow workers and company supervisors, but he could sometimes become quite nasty if he felt that discipline at work or in the classroom was too rigid. It seemed he was really serious about mastering the trade, but did not like to waste time on subjects he did not consider essential. Near the end of his second year as an apprentice he was drafted and went into the Army for two years.

After his discharge from the Army, Bob returned to his job as an apprentice, but before he went to work he made an appearance before the Joint Apprenticeship Committee and demanded that he be given credit on his apprenticeship for time spent in the Army. He claimed to have done craft-related work during the entire two years. An obvious exaggeration, but he was given credit for one and one-half years of service—which meant that he had less than two years to go to graduate to journeyman.

Just over a year later, when his class came up for graduation, Bob asked to be allowed to take the examination for journeyman. Permission was granted, and to the surprise of everyone he passed the examination with ease. It has always been the custom in the building trades to give men who have served in the armed forces a break, but Bob received more of a break than most. Part of it came about because Bob had a sort of half-belligerent, wheedling attitude that was hard to resist, plus the fact that he had worked very hard to qualify. In view of later developments, maybe charisma is the word that best describes Bob Y.

When Bob graduated to journeyman he acquired the right to a voice at union meetings, the right to vote at union elections, and to hold office in his local union. He lost no time in making use of these rights and soon plunged into local union political activities. He was a forceful speaker and often critical of union policy and union officials. Those harassing tactics soon won him a following among the younger union members. Bob worked hard, played harder, and would fight at the drop of a hat, but something about him commanded respect. He developed into a really skilled mechanic and was promoted to a job as foreman in the shop where he worked.

In the first union election, after he became eligible to hold office, Bob ran for office as a member of the Executive Board and won by a substantial margin over his nearest opponent. He served a two-year term on the Executive Board and did his job well. He attended all meetings of the board and all membership meetings as well. He was often in opposition to other members of the board and other local union officials. It was said he was much too radical for his own good and for the good of the local union.

At election time local union members were in one of those "throw-the-rascals-out" moods, and deservedly or not the incumbent Business Manager and his assistant were due to be beaten. (Those are the two full-time paid officials for most local unions of the building trades.) An older man with many years of experience in union politics and local union management was sure to be elected Business Manager, although many local union members thought he was too conservative. In any case, he was a shrewd union politician and firmed up his position by asking

Bob Y. to join forces with him. No one was surprised when the older man was elected, and Bob was elected to the position of Assistant Business Manager.

The membership of the local union were still in a troubled mood after the election, and newly elected officials were soon the target for much criticism. The new Business Manager was conservative and slow to take action, but Bob Y. suffered from no such liability. In a very short time it became apparent that he was usurping the power of his chief.

For reasons that were not quite clear the Business Manager did not seem to resent the intrusion. In fact, he appeared to be quite willing to have Bob take over. Bob was soon setting all local union policy and leading negotiations for a new three-year contract or working agreement. He quarreled with employer members of the Contractors' Association and called a couple of wildcat strikes. The strikes caused the contractors to appeal to the national union, and the general organizer for the district came in for a conference, on orders from the national union officials. The organizer made it quite clear that Bob's local union must honor its agreements or have its charter suspended.

Bob must have learned something from the experience, and from that point on he was somewhat less truculent in his attitude. He continued to act for the Business Manager and became a delegate to state association meetings and the District Council. At the end of his two-year term, no one was surprised when he ran for the office of Business Manager and was elected. For the next several years Bob Y. gave the local union strong leadership and won the respect of the entire membership. Now, at age 32, Bob Y. is showing signs of maturity. The smile is not quite so quick these days, but seems a bit more friendly and tolerant. In fact, scarcely a trace remains of the old disdainful sneer that once annoyed so many people.

No one knows what goals Bob Y. has set for himself, but it is not likely he will be content to remain for long as the chief official of a medium-sized local union. From the very beginning of his career his moves had power and purpose, with little lost motion in his drive for success. It is not likely that Bob will change his tactics now, and it would be a good bet that his name will become well known in local and national union circles. He could move up to a job with the national union, into labor relations work, or other fields, but if he should decide to stay where he is, $20,000 per year, plus liberal fringe benefits, is not bad at all.

The Tommy H. Story

Tommy H. was a good student in high school, with a well-defined talent for cartooning and commercial art work. He fully intended to go on to college and the study of commercial art, but the summer after graduation from high school he got a job as a helper on a large construction project. (To get the job it was necessary to obtain a permit of temporary membership from the local union for that trade.)

While on the job Tommy became acquainted with several other young men who were working on permits from the local unions. As the time neared for school to start, and with the construction project in its closing phase, Tommy and two of his friends decided to join the Army. They reasoned that they would have to do military service sooner or later, so why not sooner and get it out of the way? Besides, the freedom of action, the excitement, and the good wages paid on construction work made school look pretty tame by comparison.

Tommy served two years in the Army, and along the way he acquired a wife. At the time of his discharge from the Army his wife was pregnant, and he was faced with the need to provide a home and livelihood for his wife and family-to-be. Tommy did not learn a trade in the Army, and with the exception of the summer on the construction job, his work record was pretty skimpy: part-time lawnmower, box boy at a local grocery store, and other odd jobs.

Tommy, however, was a resourceful young man and had no

The installation of seating provides work for many building trades mechanics. The sports arena in New York's new Madison Square Garden, shown here, is typical.

intention of taking a job at casual labor, with low pay and no chance for advancement. He had liked the work he did that summer on construction, and the friend who had sponsored him for the first work permit was willing to recommend him for an apprenticeship with his local union. This man was a respected member of a building trades union, and his recommendation carried weight. Construction work happened to be in an up-phase at that time, Tommy was able to pass all tests and examinations, and in a short time he was working as a probationary apprentice. (At the end of six months, with a satisfactory record, Tommy would be initiated into the local union.)

Tommy was dispatched to a large shop that handled a variety of work, including large commercial and industrial projects. Tommy served his entire five-year apprenticeship there and graduated to journeyman with good, but not exceptional, grades. He was well liked by his fellow workers, was a good worker, and very good at reading blueprints and working drawings of all types.

Tommy was not, however, what could be called a really fine mechanic on jobs that required working with the tools of the trade. Good enough to get by, but he had no real aptitude for such work, and was not really happy in it. By that time he had three children, and when his father-in-law offered to take him into the family business, he quit construction and moved back to his wife's home town.

That seemed like a good idea at the time, but the relationship didn't work out. Personality clashes played a part, but the real problem was the type of work that had to be done, and few small business operations can produce the income equal to the wages Tommy had received as a journeyman mechanic. He decided to go back into construction work.

At that time, a few years after the Korean war, the United States was starting to build missile bases and test facilities on a large scale. That type of construction differed in many ways from conventional construction methods, and building trades craftsmen were faced with a need to master a new set of skills and new approaches to construction technology.

On new construction craftsmen are required to work from blueprints, and the ability to read such prints, plans, and schematic drawings is a must for any mechanic who hopes to advance to supervisor or the ownership of his own contracting business. Many of the blueprints are too large to be taken into the field and must be broken down into small sections, or working drawings. Some working drawings are schematic, whereas others present plan, elevation, or sectional views. Many of the drawings used for the installation of mechanical systems are isometric, meaning they show the work to be installed much as it will appear after it has been put in place.

Skilled mechanical draftsmen are in short supply, and with so much detail drawing to be done on a large construction job, it is often necessary to call on the skills of craftsmen who have shown aptitude for such work. Tommy H., with his talent for commercial art, had a clearly defined aptitude for detailing in the mechanical drawing field, and soon after he returned to construction work he was asked to prepare a few sample sketches. The drawings turned out to be clear and easy to read, with all dimensions accurately expressed, and indicated a notable grasp of the basic principles involved. Tommy was offered a job in the field engineering office at a foreman's rate of pay.

For the first time in his life, Tommy H. was working at a job he really liked and one that allowed him to fulfill his potential. With a five-year apprenticeship behind him, followed by nearly four years of seasoning on construction projects, the payoff was overdue. His employer soon learned that Tommy's ability was not limited to mechanical drawing and that he had a flair for estimating, material takeoff, and purchasing.

Tommy H. has now been with that contracting and engineering company for several years and he could be a top-level field supervisor. In fact, he has served in that capacity, but he prefers office work. He now has draftsmen and other craftsmen doing the detail drawing and routine work, but if a situation comes up in which it is difficult to show a section of work by standard drafting practices—which is not unusual—Tommy can always draw an artist's conception to be used as a model.

The Marty V. Story

Marty V. was a handsome boy, well built and above average height. In high school he was a fair, but sometimes erratic, student. He was a fine athlete, but was often on the verge of losing his right to compete when his grades dropped too low. He liked the attention he received as a star performer on the athletic field, but he liked off-field play even better. On several occasions when his grades dropped too low, he was warned, and tutoring was arranged, but he was never secure.

He did, however, manage to hang on until the start of his last semester, but at that time he was involved in a scandal and was suspended for several weeks. He was reinstated near the end of the term, but the lost time had caused him to lose credits, and he lacked a few units. Marty was not able to graduate with his class.

Marty's father was a long-standing and respected member of a local union of the building trades. He was able to sponsor Marty for an apprenticeship, but not in his own craft. Marty's application for an apprenticeship was accepted, but with certain reservations. He would be required to complete his high-school education, and his probationary period would be carefully supervised. Marty was strong, willing to work, and, when his interest was aroused, an intelligent worker. He completed his high-school work and behaved quite well during the six-month probationary period. At the end of that period he was initiated into the union as an apprentice member.

A few months later, however, the Joint Apprenticeship Committee received some rather disturbing reports on Marty. The reports revealed that he was often absent from his job, was not attending the apprentice-training classes, and would not accept the discipline of senior mechanics on the job. He was called before the Joint Apprenticeship Committee for a warning and reprimand. His attitude must improve or he would be dropped from the apprentice program and the union.

Marty did show an improved attitude for a while, but a few months later he was arrested for driving while under the influence of alcohol, and his driver's license was suspended. The loss of a driver's license is a serious matter, for apprentices are often required to drive a shop truck. The Joint Apprenticeship Committee was inclined to drop Marty, but, out of respect for his father, he was given another chance. With help from the committee he was able to get a limited driver's license that allowed him to drive during working hours.

Marty did behave somewhat better after the arrest incident, but he was not exactly a credit to himself or to his local union. He had been fired from several shops, and it was becoming difficult for the union to place him on a job. Near the end of his fourth year as an apprentice, Marty was assigned to work with a heliarc welder. That type of welding is not new, but it is coming into wider use each year. From the craftsman's point of view heliarc welding has certain advantages over conventional electric arc welding. The work is cleaner, and the welder does not have to wear heavy protective clothing. In addition, heliarc welding is usually done in a section of the shop that is set off from other workers and work activities. Each welder, and his helper, has his own enclosed work area.

Marty took to heliarc welding from the first day. The welder he was assigned to help noted his interest and made an effort to explain the setting up of the equipment. Later he allowed Marty to practice a bit during the lunch hour and at odd moments when time was open. Marty kept the equipment in good order and was very attentive to the needs of his welder.

Later that year, when the fall school classes started, Marty was first in line to sign up for the heliarc welding class. It is an optional subject, but an apprentice is given full credit in his apprentice training. He studied the texts and was very attentive during the lecture periods. When his turn came to do some actual heliarc welding he wanted to stay with it after his allotted time had elapsed. In fact, he had to be forced to relinquish the welding booth and the equipment.

From that time on, Marty never missed a training session and he took advantage of every opportunity to get in some extra practice. By the time he graduated to journeyman he was a pretty fair heliarc welder, with a good grasp of layout work and blueprint reading. At this time he has been working as a journeyman heliarc welder for three years.

Since he has found what appears to be his niche in the building trades, Marty V. is a happy and well-adjusted man. He is on the job every day and gets along well with fellow employees and supervisors. No one has taken the trouble to find out just why Marty V. took to heliarc welding, but it may have been the fact that he works in comparative isolation. Maybe he likes having his own little sanctuary.

The Bill J. Story

The local unions of the building trades like the idea of maintaining membership by taking in young men on the apprentice level, which means most men will be in the under-25 age bracket. That does not mean older men are denied the right to join a building trades union. On the contrary, many men who have learned a trade outside of union jurisdiction have found a road to a better way of life and more rewarding financial returns by joining a union after they have achieved the journeyman level of education and training.

Bill J. was in that category and had worked for years as a helper, journeyman, operator, and supervisor in oil refining. At the age of 40 he had worked up to the position of superintendent in a small independent oil-refining plant. It was a good job, but it was the end of the line. There was no chance for further advancement, because that was the highest position open with the company to a man with his experience and educational background. Bill J. is a man with boundless energy and capacity for work. He could never be content to remain on a job with no chance for advancement and no increasing challenges to meet.

The opportunity for Bill to break out of his rut came when his employer decided to revise existing refining facilities and build an addition. The work was done by a contracting and engineering company, and the craftsmen employed by the company were members of building trades local unions. Bill had a chance to observe the men at work and he liked the way they went at the job, their skill with tools, and their general job know-how. During the job Bill became friends with several of the craftsmen and found out how they had become members of the union. Some had served a formal apprenticeship, but others had learned their trade outside of union jurisdiction. All information was freely given, and Bill was surprised to learn that with his wide experience in refinery maintenance, repair, and operation, he might be able to qualify for membership in the union of his choice.

Bill induced one of his new friends to act as sponsor when he made application for union membership, and his application was approved by the union Investigating Committee. A few weeks later he was instructed to appear before the local union Examining Board. Bill made good use of the intervening time to brush up on shop mathematics, blueprint reading, and other subjects. He also read a few books relating to the trade. The effort paid off, and he passed the examination with ease.

Bill was initiated into the union, and his name was placed on the out-of-work (availability) list. Shortly thereafter he was dispatched to a large new chemical plant that was under construction. A chemical plant is similar in many respects to an oil refinery, so Bill was on familiar ground. He could read blueprints, understand a bill-of-material, and find his way around the construction site.

Bill was a good worker, knew how to get along with men,

and he was ambitious. In less than three months he was promoted to foreman and his pay on the new job was higher than the salary he had received as a refinery superintendent, plus substantial fringe benefits.

The job lasted two years, and when the contractor moved out they asked Bill to stay on the payroll as a supervisor. He accepted and became a permanent employee of a highly respected construction contractor. Bill served in a number of capacities and after two years was given a chance to supervise all men of his craft on a multi-million-dollar construction project. He was responsible for the work activities of several general foremen, twenty foremen, and up to 150 journeyman mechanics. A lot of responsibility and a lot of work, but Bill thrived on it.

When that project was completed, Bill was transferred to the foreign division and assigned to a job in Colombia, South America. On all supervisory jobs up to that time he had been responsible for the work activities of men of his own craft. On the new job he would supervise the activities of all building trades craftsmen employed on the project. Bill got along fine and, when the project was completed, was assigned to a job in Puerto Rico.

After the Puerto Rico project was completed, Bill was sent to a construction job in Mexico where his employer was building refining facilities for the Mexican government. In Mexico, and in nearly all other foreign countries, they try to reserve all employment opportunities for their own nationals. A contractor is allowed to bring in only a few key men. Bill got along well on that job, and when the project manager had to return to the States for medical treatment, he assumed full responsibility.

Bill J. never took a very active part in local union activities, possibly because he was away from his home local most of the time. As a top-level supervisor he is not required to have a union card, but he has found it good policy to keep up his union membership. Bill runs a strict job, whether in the States or on a foreign job, but he has a reputation for fair dealing, and that is a valuable asset for any man in such a position.

Bill is smart enough to know that he must have skilled craftsmen to get his jobs done. He also knows that the local unions have a large pool of skilled mechanics. He also knows that hard-working, fully qualified craftsmen can make him look good. He shows his appreciation by maintaining good labor relations at all times and does not try to hog the credit. With that sort of reputation, he attracts the best men in every craft to his jobs. He always tries to make his crews look good and his policy is known the world over wherever construction men gather. Good men will go far to work under such conditions.

The James G. Story

When he got out of school, the first job James G. held was that of helper in the maintenance and repair department on a large naval weapons base in the desert area of the western United States. The job was under U.S. Civil Service and it seemed a fine opportunity for a man who had completed only two years of high school. The job would be steady, the pay was fair, and there would be chance for advancement in grade.

James did advance in grade, but progress was slow and it took him fifteen years to work up from helper to 1st Grade mechanic. James was married and had three children, which is really what brought about the crisis that forced a change in his career. Housing is often scarce on those isolated bases and it is allotted on the basis of rank, rather than need. The James G. family had lived in some pretty bad quarters over the years, but now that he had achieved the grade of mechanic 1st Class he would move up on the housing priority list.

Many armed services installations that offer jobs for mechanics under Civil Service, such as the one where James was employed, are subject to a boom-and-bust cycle similar to that found in the construction industry. At any given moment a base may have a top priority rating, but a few months later as projects hit a peak and start to phase out, priority ratings may fall.

Such a base might stay in the low priority class for a year or two until new projects are assigned.

Shortly after James was promoted to 1st Grade mechanic, the base where he worked was forced into one of those downswings. For a while it was just a rumor, but the word finally came out that a large part of the facility was to be deactivated. That would mean many changes, and employees would be laid off or transferred. James had enough seniority so that he was in no danger of being laid off, but he might be transferred or have to take a lower rating for a time. In any case the family would be uprooted and a long period of uncertainty would ensue.

A few weeks later, official notice came that James would be transferred to another base. He had three choices of job location, and all were in isolated and undesirable areas. It was a severe blow to James G. and his wife, as they had hoped to be able to move to an area with a better choice of housing and schools. James was discouraged and considered quitting his job, but was reluctant to give up his seniority, retirement benefits, and hard-won 1st Class rating.

A family conference was held and it was decided that James would make an effort to find another job, but no drastic action would be taken. James went alone to the nearest town of any size, which happened to be a thriving city with a population in excess of 100,000. The city had been expanding industrially for several years and it appeared that it would continue to do so.

James made his first stop at the office of the State Employment Service. During the interview he discussed every aspect of his problem with the counselor, and between them they worked out a two-phase course of action. The first phase, which was for the long pull, called for James to make application with every city, county, state, and federal Civil Service Commission that might offer jobs for men with his skills. The second, and short-range phase, called for James to make the rounds of every employer in the area who was known to hire men of his trade.

With the help of the counselor, James made a list of all potential employers and the following day started on his rounds. He made many calls with no success and by the end of the third day he was ready to give up, but on his last call of the day he talked to the personnel manager of an independent oil-refining company. The employment manager told James that his company did not do its own maintenance and repair work, but sublet it to a contractor. He also told James that his company was about to start a large overhaul and revision job that would take several months to complete. He advised James to apply for a job with that contractor and was able to set up an interview by telephone.

James had a pleasant interview with the employment manager for the contractor, who listened attentively as he detailed his experience. The employment manager asked a lot of questions and then asked James when he would be available for work. When he recovered from the shock, James explained that he would have to give notice to his present employer and find a place to live. He thought thirty days would be enough time, and this date was satisfactory with the contractor.

The personnel manager then informed James that he would have to become a member of a local union for the building and construction trades. At that bit of news James was again almost thrown into a state of shock. He had had no previous experience with labor unions, but was under the impression that they did not welcome new members. The personnel manager told James he had been misinformed and had nothing to fear. The job he was offered was under the Metal Trades Division of the local union and the conditions for membership were quite different than they would be for a man who wanted to get into the Building Trades Division of the union.

Under a metal trades agreement with a local union for the building trades, a contractor has a right to hire any man he chooses, with the provision that all men thus hired make application for membership in the union within a stated period. The personnel manager advised James to go directly to the office of the local union and gave him a letter to the union Business Manager stating his intention to hire James as a maintenance mechanic.

Except for the fact that he had to wait until the next day for an interview with the Business Manager, there were no problems. James filled out his application for membership; paid one third of the initiation fee, and arranged to pay the balance over a period of six months. He was given a copy of the local union constitution and by-laws and was told that he would be notified when to appear for initiation. There would be no qualifying examination for the Metal Trades Division, but at the end of three years James would be eligible to take the examination to qualify as a journeyman mechanic in the Building Trades Division of the local union. A few weeks after starting on the new job, James was initiated into the union at an open membership meeting.

James gave notice, as required under Civil Service rules, and had his name put on the inactive list. That would make him eligible for reinstatement at his old rate if things did not go well on the new job. He did not, at that time, draw the money that had accumulated in his retirement fund, which would make it easier if he decided to return to U.S. Civil Service. James is not apt to go back to his old way of life. He likes the work on his new job and attends many journeyman-training classes that are offered by the local union and the local school system. At the end of the required three years of membership in the Metal Trades Division he will take the examination to qualify as a building trades journeyman mechanic, with every expectation that he will be able to achieve his goal.

When James does graduate to the Building Trades Division, that does not mean he will be forced to change employers. The contractor he works for also does new construction work. The pay rates for metal trades journeymen may run as much as 20 percent below those paid in the Building Trades Division. One other important reason for qualifying as a building trades jour-

In renovating several identical rooms, precut flooring material saves time and minimizes waste material.

neyman is that a building trades journeyman can work on either metal trades or building trades jobs, whereas a man with a Metal Trades Division card can work only on metal trades jobs. (*Note:* That is a very important point for men who seek jobs in the building trades, and who are not in too much of a hurry.)

Any man who serves an apprenticeship and masters a trade can be sure of two things: He will never have to work at common labor or on menial jobs, and he will be in an earning bracket in which he will have a chance to build an estate of property and money. In addition he will be able to lay the foundation for a lifetime of rewarding work activity. Any man who can generate enough interest in his career to gain a feeling of satisfaction and achievement in his work will have a worthwhile estate in his vocation. In most instances the estate of property will follow as a matter of course. Charley C. is a little older than the other men cited in the foregoing case histories, but his career does inject a personal element into the subject. His story is not unusual.

The Charley C. Story
Charley C. was born in the Midwest, but moved to the West Coast with his family the year before he graduated from high school. His first full-time job was as a helper in a large shipyard. The shipbuilding industry had been in a slump since the end of World War II, but there was always some repair and conversion work to be done.

Charley was fascinated by ships, the pay was pretty good, and he had become a member of a building trades local union, Metal Trades Division. He worked as a helper for three years and then qualified as a metal trades journeyman mechanic. Shortly after the Korean war started, Charley enlisted in the Navy. He served three years and was discharged in late 1955. He returned to his job at the shipyard and was promoted to foreman a few months later.

Charley had always taken an interest in union activities. Soon after his discharge from the Navy, he ran for, and was elected, a member of the Executive Board for the Metal Trades Division. He served two terms, of two years each, on the Executive Board and then decided to run for the office of Business Agent. His local union had five Business Agents, but only one was to be elected for the Metal Trades Division. Five men ran for this office, and Charley won by a very narrow margin.

Charley worked hard at his job, and his first two-year term passed quickly. When he ran for a second term it is significant to note that he won by a substantial majority over the other candidates. In the years that followed the slump in shipbuilding after World War II, and again after the Korean war, the labor unions had tended to forget about the Metal Trades Division and concentrated their efforts in what appeared to be more promising areas.

Charley C. did not go along with that philosophy and did all that he could to better the wages and working conditions of the metal trades craftsmen. He acted as negotiator on all metal trades working agreements and "hung tough" on every issue. On one occasion he deadlocked negotiations for several weeks, until he finally won a few concessions for the men he represented. It was said that he wore down his fellow negotiators and management by sheer persistence. Over the years Charley was responsible for winning many improvements for the men of the shipbuilding industry. In the process he won the respect of his own members, other labor unions, and management representatives.

Now, after more than twelve years in office, Charley is elected term after term and could probably stay there for life. He is a friendly, easygoing man, and his attitude sometimes leads people to believe he is a soft touch. They soon learn that he can be decisive and forceful when the need arises. He has a private office, but the door is seldom closed.

The job pays pretty well, though not as much as an equivalent job in the Building Trades Division of his union. However, with fringe benefits, expenses, and the use of a car, his total income might exceed $18,000 per year—but not for a 40-hour week! Seventy hours might be closer to the mark, which is not unusual for paid local union officials.

If Charley C. ever failed to get reelected, which is not likely, he could move into a good job in labor relations or as personnel manager for one of the large shipbuilding companies. For the sake of the men that he represents, and for the labor movement in general, it is to be hoped he will never accept one of the attractive job offers he has received.

It has truly been said, "Man does not live by bread alone," and that is true of every life. The estate that Charley C. has accumulated appears to be prosperous and well balanced in all areas.

CHAPTER XII

General Information

The National Unions

The building and Construction Trades Department of the AFL–CIO is made up of fourteen national unions that represent approximately 3,500,000 skilled craftsmen and apprentices. Those national unions have a network of local unions that covers every section of the United States and Canada. The title, mailing address, number of members, number of local unions, and publications for each national union will be included in the information given in this chapter.

Information on such subjects as apprenticeships, jurisdiction of work, and membership requirements can be obtained by writing to the national union for each trade, or at the office of the local union. The local unions are listed in the telephone directory. Each national union has a title that includes every aspect of its jurisdiction, but is usually known by a more common name. For the sake of easy identification, the common name of each national union title will be given in italics.

International Association of Heat & Frost Insulators and *Asbestos Workers:*
    1300 Connecticut Avenue, N.W., Washington, D.C.
    13,700 members, 124 local unions. Publication: *Asbestos Worker,* quarterly.

International Brotherhood of *Boilermakers,* Iron Shipbuilders, Blacksmiths, Forgers and Helpers:
    Eighth Avenue at State Street, Kansas City, Kansas

150,750 members, 475 local unions. Publication: *Boiler-maker-Blacksmith Record*, monthly.

Bricklayers, Masons and Plasterers' International Union of America:
815 15th Street, N.W., Washington, D.C. 20006
158,792 members, 957 local unions. Publication: *Bricklayer, Mason and Plasterer*, monthly.

Laborers' International Union of North America:
905 16th Street, N.W., Washington, D.C.
476,598 members, 955 local unions. Publication: *Laborer*, monthly.

United Brotherhood of *Carpenters* and Joiners of America:
101 Constitution Avenue, N.W., Washington, D.C. 20001
863,000 members, 2,900 local unions. Publication: *The Carpenter*, monthly.

International Brotherhood of *Electrical* Workers:
1200 15th Street, N.W., Washington, D.C.
800,000 members, 1,800 local unions. Publication: *Electrical Workers Journal*, monthly.

International Union of *Elevator* Constructors:
1200 South 12th Street, Room 1515, Philadelphia, Pennsylvania 19107
12,000 members, 107 local unions. Publication: *Elevator Constructor*, monthly.

International union of *Operating Engineers:*
1125 17th Street, N.W., Washington, D.C. 20036
284,700 members, 343 local unions. Publication: *International Operating Engineer*, monthly.

International Association of Bridge, Structural and Ornamental *Ironworkers:*
3615 Olive Street, St. Louis, Missouri 63108

146,362 members, 326 local unions. Publication: *Ironworker,* monthly.

Wood, Wire and Metal *Lathers'* International Union:
  6530 New Hampshire Avenue, Takoma Park, Maryland 20012
  18,000 members, 303 local unions. Publication: *The Lather,* monthly.

International Association of *Marble,* Slate and Stone Polishers, Rubbers and Sawyers; Tile and Marble Setters' Helpers and Marble, Mosaic and Terrazzo Workers' Helpers:
  821 15th Street, N.W., Washington, D.C.
  10,000 members, 125 local unions.

Industrial Union of *Marine* and Shipbuilding Workers of America:
  534 Cooper Street, Camden, New Jersey
  30,000 members, 42 local unions. Publication: *Shipbuilder,* monthly.

Brotherhood of *Painters,* Decorators and Paperhangers of America:
  217–19 North Sixth Street, Lafayette, Indiana 47901
  201,000 members, 1,208 local unions. Publication: *Painter & Decorator,* monthly.

Operative *Plasterers* & Cement Masons International Association of the United States and Canada:
  1125 17th Street, N.W., Washington, D.C.
  70,000 members, 550 local unions. Publication: *Plasterer and Cement Mason,* monthly.

United Association of Journeymen and Apprentices of the *Plumbing* and Pipefitting Industry of the United States and Canada:
  901 Massachusetts Avenue, N.W., Washington, D.C. 20001
  285,000 members, 725 local unions. Publication: *United Association Journal,* monthly.

Sheet Metal Workers' International Association:
  1000 Connecticut Avenue, N.W., Washington, D.C. 20036
  85,000 members, 535 local unions. Publication: *Sheet Metal Workers Journal,* monthly.

United *Slate* Tile and Composition *Roofers* Damp and Waterproof Workers Association:
  1125 17th Street, N.W., Washington, D.C. 20036
  25,000 members, 275 local unions. Publication: *Journeyman Roofer and Waterproofer,* monthly.

In addition to the national unions for the building and construction trades a number of national and international organizations are good sources of information for anyone interested in the field. They are:

Building and Construction Trades Department of AFL–CIO:
  815 16th Street, N.W., Washington, D.C.
  3,500,000 members, 635 local and state chapters. Publications: *Building and Construction Trades Bulletin,* monthly. *Construction Craftsman,* monthly.

This federation includes asbestos workers, bricklayers, masons, plasterers, carpenters, electrical workers, elevator constructors, operating engineers, granite cutters, hod carriers, common laborers, carpet and tile layers, tile and stone workers, painters and decorators, paperhangers, plumbers and pipefitters, roofers, and other related trades.

Construction Industry Joint Council:
  1012 14th Street, N.W., Washington, D.C. 20005
  Representatives of eighteen national and international unions affiliated with the Building and Construction Trades Department of the AFL–CIO, and representatives of various national general and specialty contractors associations. The purpose of the groups

is to promote the welfare of the building and construction industry in the public interest and to provide a forum for discussion of labor-management and industry problems. Cost of operating is divided equally between contractors and unions.

Metal Trades Department of AFL–CIO:
815 16th Street, N.W., Washington, D.C. 20006
Federation of labor unions in fields of metals manufacturing, fabrication, and processing, including boilermakers, carpenters, chemical workers, iron workers, metal polishers, pattern makers, molders, sheet metal workers, and similar crafts. Publication: *Bulletin of the Metal Trades Department,* monthly.

Besides the national unions for the building trades and the federations of national unions, combined with certain contractor associations, are many local, state, and national associations that have a stake in everything that affects the building and construction industry, including education, training, manpower recruitment, and public relations. In most instances the name of the organization indicates the field of interest. Most such organizations have state and local chapters, and the addresses can be found in the city directory or telephone directory. For the sake of brevity, no description of activities for each group will be given, except as stated above.

Associated General Contractors of America:
Munsey Trust Building, Washington, D.C.

National Association of Home Builders:
1625 "L" Street, N.W., Washington, D.C.

National Joint Apprentice and Training Committee for the Electrical Industry:
1200 18th Street, N.W., Washington, D.C. 20036

Painting and Decorating Contractors Association of America:
2625 West Peterson Avenue, Chicago, Illinois 60605

National Association of Plumbing Contractors:
1016 20th Street, N.W., Washington, D.C. 20036

Mechanical Contractors Association of America:
2 Pennsylvania Plaza, Suite 1950, New York, N.Y. 10001

National Roofing Contractors Association:
300 West Washington Street, Chicago, Illinois 60606

Sheet Metal & Air Conditioning Contractors National Association:
1611 North Kent Street, Arlington, Virginia 22209

American Society of Heating, Refrigeration & Air Conditioning Engineers:
345 East 47th Street, New York, N.Y. 10017

Consulting Engineers Council:
Madison Building, Suite 713, 1155 15th Street, N.W., Washington, D.C. 20005

Air Conditioning and Refrigeration Institute:
1815 North Fort Meyer Drive, Arlington, Virginia 22209

Government Jobs for Building Trades Craftsmen
Many agencies of the U.S. Government offer jobs for helpers, apprentices, and journeymen in occupations that require knowledge and experience in building and construction skills. The jobs are open at Army, Navy, Air Force, and General Service Administration installations.

The jobs are offered through the U.S. Civil Service Commission, and every job opening must be announced publicly, though many job bulletins are given only local circulation. No single announcement list is published for all Civil Service job openings, but information can be obtained at post offices, state employment offices, school counseling offices, and similar places.

In addition to those sources of information, the main office of the U.S. Civil Service Commission in Washington, D.C., will respond to a letter or postcard with information and application forms in time to apply for most jobs. For information, write to any of the following sources:

United States Civil Service Commission:
Washington, D.C. 20025

U.S. Civil Service Commission, Regional Office:
240 Peachtree Street, N.W., Atlanta, Georgia 30303. This office serves Alabama, Florida, Georgia, Mississippi, North Carolina, South Carolina, Tennessee, Puerto Rico, and the Virgin Islands.

U.S. Civil Service Commission, Regional Office:
Post Office and Courthouse Building, Boston, Massachusetts 02100
Serves Connecticut, Maine, Massachusetts, New Hampshire, Rhode Island, and Vermont.

U.S. Civil Service Commission, Regional Office:
Main Post Office Building, Chicago, Illinois 60607. Serves Illinois, Indiana, Kentucky, Michigan, Ohio, and Wisconsin.

U.S. Civil Service Commission, Regional Office:
1114 Commerce Street, Dallas, Texas 75202. Serves Arkansas, Louisiana, Oklahoma, and Texas.

U.S. Civil Service Commission, Regional Office:
Building 41, Federal Center, Denver, Colorado 80225. Serves Arizona, Colorado, New Mexico, Utah, and Wyoming.

U.S. Civil Service Commission, Regional Office:
220 East 42nd Street, New York, N.Y. 10017. Serves New York and New Jersey.

U.S. Civil Service Commission, Regional Office:
Customhouse, Philadelphia, Pennsylvania 19106. Serves Delaware, Maryland, Pennsylvania, Virginia, and West Virginia.

U.S. Civil Service Commission, Regional Office:
1256 Federal Building, St. Louis, Missouri 63103. Serves Iowa, Kansas, Minnesota, Missouri, Nebraska, North Dakota, and South Dakota.

U.S. Civil Service Commission, Regional Office:
Federal Office Building, San Francisco, California 94102. Serves California, Hawaii, Nevada, and Pacific overseas area.

U.S. Civil Service Commission, Regional Office:
302 Federal Office Building, Seattle, Washington 98104. Serves Alaska, Idaho, Montana, Oregon, and Washington.

* * * * *

The State Employment Service
Every state has a public employment office that operates local offices throughout the state. The main purpose of the agency is to help workers find jobs and to help employers find workers, as well as offering a number of other services that could be of value to any individual who wants to work as a helper, apprentice, or journeyman in the building trades and related fields. Those services include aptitude tests, vocational guidance, and job counseling. For information, write to the office nearest your place of residence.

Director, Department of Industrial Relations:
State Office Building, Montgomery, Alabama

Director, Employment Security Commission:
Box 2661, Juneau, Alaska

Administrator-Director, Arizona State Employment Service:
1720 West Madison Street, Phoenix, Arizona

Administrator, Employment Security Division Department of Labor:
Employment-Security Welfare Building, Little Rock, Arkansas
Write to Box 2981, Little Rock, Arkansas.

Director, Department of Employment:
800 Capitol Avenue, Sacramento, California

Executive Director, Department of Employment:
568 State Capitol Annex Building, Denver, Colorado

Executive Director, Employment Security Division, Department of Labor:
92 Farmington Avenue, Hartford, Connecticut

Chairman–Executive Director, Unemployment Compensation Commission:
601 Shipley Street, Wilmington, Delaware

Director, U.S. Employment Service for the District of Columbia:
1724 F Street, Washington, D.C. 20025

Chairman, Industrial Commission:
Caldwell Building, Tallahassee, Florida

Director, Employment Security Agency, Department of Labor:
State Labor Building, Atlanta, Georgia

Department of Labor and Industrial Relations:
825 Mililani Street. P.O. Box 1761, Honolulu, Hawaii

Executive Director, Employment Security Agency:
317 Main Street, Boise, Idaho. P.O. Box 520, Boise, Idaho

Commissioner of Placement and Unemployment Compensation, Department of Labor:
165 North Canal Street, Room 200, Chicago, Illinois

Director, Employment Security Division:
141 South Meridian Street, Indianapolis, Indiana

Chairman, Employment Security Commission:
112 Eleventh Street, Des Moines, Iowa

Executive Director, Executive Security Division, State Department of Labor:
401 Topeka Boulevard, Topeka, Kansas

Executive Director, Bureau of Employment Security, Department of Economic Security:
Capitol Office Building, Frankfort, Kentucky

Administrator, Division of Employment Security, Department of Labor:
Capitol Annex Building, Baton Rouge, Louisiana. P.O. Box 4094

Chairman, Employment Security Commission:
331 Water Street, Augusta, Maine

Executive Director, Department of Employment Security:
6 North Liberty Street, Baltimore, Maryland

Director, Division of Employment Security:
881 Commonwealth Avenue, Boston, Massachusetts

Director, Employment Security Commission:
514 Boulevard Building, 7310 Woodward Avenue, Detroit, Michigan

Commissioner, Department of Employment Security:
369 Cedar Street, St. Paul, Minnesota

Executive Director, Employment Security Commission:
Milner Building, Jackson, Mississippi. P.O. Box 1699

Director, Division of Employment Security, Department of Labor and Industrial Relations:
421 East Dunklin Street, Jefferson City, Missouri

Chairman & Executive Director, Unemployment Compensation Commission:
Sam W. Mitchell Building, Helena, Montana. P.O. Box 1728

Director, Division of Employment Security, Department of Labor:
134 South Twelfth Street, Lincoln, Nebraska. P.O. Box 1033

Executive Director, Employment Security Department:
P.O. Box 602,
Carson City, Nevada

Director, Division of Employment Security:
34 South Main Street, Concord, New Hampshire

Director, Division of Employment Security:
28 West State Street, Trenton, New Jersey

Chairman–Executive Director, Employment Security Commission:
103 6th Street, S.W., Albuquerque, New Mexico. P.O. Box 1799

Executive Director, Division of Employment, Department of Labor:
500 Eighth Avenue, New York, N.Y.

Chairman, Employment Security Commission:
Jones & N. McDowell Streets, Raleigh, North Carolina. P.O. Box 589

Director, North Dakota Employment Service:
207 Broadway, Bismarck, North Dakota. P.O. Box 568

Administrator, Bureau of Unemployment Compensation:
427 Cleveland Avenue, Columbus, Ohio

Executive Director, Employment Security Commission:
American National Building, Oklahoma City, Oklahoma

Administrator, Unemployment Compensation Commission:
500 Public Service Building, Salem, Oregon

Executive Director, Bureau of Employment Security, Department of Labor and Industry:
Seventh and Forster Streets, Harrisburg, Pennsylvania

Director, Puerto Rico Employment Service:
Parque Street No. 607, Santurce, San Juan, Puerto Rico

Director, Department of Employment Security:
24 Mason Street, Providence, Rhode Island

Executive Director, Employment Security Commission:
1225 Laurel Street, Columbia, South Carolina. P.O. Box 995

Commissioner, Employment Security Department:
310 Lincoln Street South, Aberdeen, South Dakota

Commissioner, Department of Employment Security:
Cordell Hull State Office Building, Nashville, Tennessee

Administrator, Texas Employment Commission:
Brown Building, Austin, Texas

Administrator, Department of Employment Security Industrial
Commission:
174 Social Hall Avenue, Salt Lake City, Utah. P.O. Box 2100

Chairman, Unemployment Compensation Commission:
7 School Street, Montpelier, Vermont

Commissioner, Unemployment Compensation Commission:
Broad-Grace Arcade, Richmond, Virginia

Director, Virgin Islands Employment Service:
Charlotte Amalie, St. Thomas, Virgin Islands

Commissioner, Employment Security Department:
Old Capitol Building, Olympia, Washington. P.O. Box 367

Director, Department of Employment Security:
State Office Building, California & Washington Streets, Charleston, West Virginia

Director, Wisconsin State Employment Service:
105 South Blair Street, Madison, Wisconsin

Executive Director, Employment Security Commission:
136½ South Wolcott Street, Casper, Wyoming. P.O. Box 760

Trade Journals and Industry Publications
When an individual makes a career decision, the effects are

long-lasting, and mistakes can be frustrating. For that reason it is of vital importance to make a careful investigation of the occupational field of interest. The investigation should include aptitude testing, vocational counseling, interviews with employers, supervisors, journeymen and apprentices who are working in the field, and field trips to construction sites for a firsthand look at what goes on during the various stages of a construction project, large or small.

In addition to all of the information sources listed in this book, one other important source should not be overlooked—the trade journals and industry publications for every trade and occupational field. Many such magazines and journals are put out for the building and construction industry and they offer the student or trainee an insight into construction methods that can be found in no other area. They bring illustrated stories about every form of construction activity, news items, technical developments, new materials, new equipment, industry gossip, and other items of interest.

A few of the publications are available on newsstands and in public libraries, but most are distributed on what is known as a "controlled-circulation" basis, which means that they are sent without charge to industry contractors, engineers, supervisors, supply-store operators, instructors, and other qualified individuals. *Most editors will send a free copy on request.* In most instances the name of the magazine will indicate the special field covered. The following list is by no means complete:

Kitchen Business, 7 East 43rd Street, New York, N.Y. 10017.

Illustrated articles show builders and architects how to sell homes through greater emphasis on kitchen equipment, cabinets, built-in appliances, and interesting design features.

Flooring, Harbrace Building, Duluth, Minnesota 55802.

For dealers and contractors in flooring installations, including hardwood, resilient, ceramic, seamless, etc.

Plastering Industries, 215 West Harrison, Seattle, Washington 98119.

Articles and news stories for the lathing and plastering industry. Covers all subjects for the field, with illustrated articles and case histories of successful operations.

Tile and Decorative Surfaces, 3421 Ocean View Boulevard, Glendale, California 91208.

Technical discussions of tile installations, new uses for tile by builders, decorators and contractors.

American Roofer and Building Improvement Contractor, 205 West Monroe Avenue, Chicago, Illinois 60606.

Publishes only exceptionally interesting stories for roofing and building improvement contractors. Articles are illustrated.

Apartment Construction News, 7 East 43rd Street, New York, N.Y. 10017.

Issued monthly for builders and developers of multifamily housing. Features include design, finance, merchandising, and management of apartments.

Building Construction, 5 South Wabash, Chicago, Illinois.

Editor uses articles and features that stress interrelationship between architects, contractors, and consulting engineers.

Building Progress, 427 6th Avenue, S.E., Cedar Rapids, Iowa 52406.

Editorial aim is to present the best new ideas and trends in the planning, construction, and decoration of all types of commercial buildings, including restaurants, hotels, motels, churches, schools, clinics, and the like.

The Central Constructor, 300 Hubbell Building, Des Moines, Iowa 50309.

Official publication for the Associated General Contractors of Iowa. Covers all areas of construction and association news.

Central States Construction Magazine, 4125 Gage Center Drive, Topeka, Kansas 66604.

Of interest to building, heavy construction, highway construction, and land improvement contractors in Kansas and Western Missouri.

Construction Equipments Operation & Maintenance, 220 Higley Building, Cedar Rapids, Iowa 52401.

For users of heavy construction equipment, with articles and features on use, operation, and maintenance of heavy construction equipment, job safety, and so forth.

Contractor News, 56th and Chestnut Streets, Philadelphia, Pennsylvania 19139.

For professional building contractors and subcontractors. Publishes articles on such subjects as liability insurance, bonding, estimating methods, bidding procedures, cost control, and expediting methods.

Excavating Contractor, 200 James Street, Barrington, Illinois 60010.

Articles on maintenance of earth-moving equipment; any type of unusual excavating jobs, business, and bookkeeping methods.

Highway Builder, 600 North Third Street, Harrisburg, Pennsylvania 17101.

Publishes stories about highway and bridge construction projects in Pennsylvania and bordering states.

Mid-west Contractor, P.O. Box 766, Kansas City, Missouri 64141.

Articles about large construction contracts in Iowa, Nebraska, Kansas, and Missouri. Better construction methods, material handling, labor relations, etc.

Modern Steel Construction, American Institute of Steel Construction, 101 Park Avenue, New York, N.Y. 10017.

Articles, pictures, and diagrams of new steel-frame buildings and bridges; new designs, new developments, etc.

Western Construction, 609 Mission Street, San Francisco, California 94105.

Published for heavy construction contractors and job supervisors. Uses articles on street, highway, bridge, tunnel, and dam construction in thirteen Western States.

World Construction, 466 Lexington Avenue, New York, N.Y. 10017.

Issued monthly to English-speaking engineers, contractors, and government officials in the Eastern Hemisphere. Uses articles that stress how contractors can get jobs done faster, better, and cheaper.

Welding Engineering, P.O. Box 28, Morton Grove, Illinois 60053.

Publishes articles on welding and related processes for industry, production, construction, and maintenance. Uses photos and drawings to show interesting welding and cutting operations.

Air Conditioning, Heating and Refrigeration News, P.O. Box 6000, Birmingham, Michigan 49012.

This weekly publication is probably the most widely quoted publication for the field. Editorial coverage is broad, and readership is worldwide.

Domestic Engineering, 1801 South Prairie Avenue, Chicago, Illinois 60616.

Illustrated articles on management, marketing, and technical subjects for mechanical contractors, with emphasis on sheet metal work, heating, and air conditioning.

Snips Magazine, 5707 West Lake Street, Chicago, Illinois 60644.

Publication covers every phase of sheet metal fabrication and installation, air conditioning, heating, roofing, etc. *Snips* book and letter shop is an excellent source of technical books for the construction industry.

Plant Engineering, 308 East James Street, Barrington, Illinois 60010.

This illustrated monthly goes to plant engineers in every part of the world. Primary coverage of all maintenance, operation, and repair activities in large plants.

Refrigeration Service and Contracting, 2720 Des Plaines Avenue, Des Plaines, Illinois 60018.

This is the official publication of the Refrigeration Service Engineers Society. The chief purpose of the publication, and the society, is the education and training of technicians and mechanics for the air conditioning, heating, and refrigeration fields.

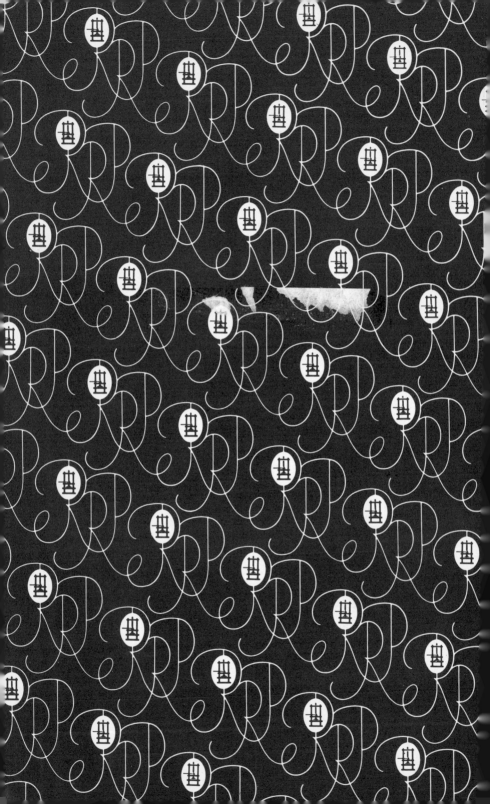